INTRODUCT ION

In the powerful domain of business, where rivalry is furious and purchaser assumptions are steadily developing, the specialty of personalization in promoting arose as a reference point of advancement. Meet Rachel Streams, a visionary promoting leader who explored the fierce waters of the business with a versatile soul and an immovable obligation to changing the client experience.

Rachel's process started in the core of a clamoring city, where she joined a groundbreaking web based business startup. Not at all like the traditional "sometime in the distant past" stories, this story unfurls in the speedy present, where Rachel wrestled with the test of associating with a group of people suffocating in an ocean of nonexclusive publicizing.

Powered by an unquenchable interest and an inborn longing to comprehend her clients, Rachel set out on a journey for a game-evolving arrangement. She dove profound into information investigation, perceiving that each snap, each buy, and each association held the way to opening the singular inclinations of her clients.

Rachel began a life-changing journey of personalization as she deciphered the intricate patterns woven into the data. At this point not happy with projecting a wide net, she imagined fitting encounters that reverberated with the extraordinary goals and wants of every client.

The advancement came as man-made reasoning and AI. Rachel, with a sharp eye for development, saddled these innovations to make calculations that could anticipate client inclinations with uncanny precision. The showcasing scene was an at this point not an immense, unfamiliar area; it turned into a close dance between the brand and the person.

In a significant second, Rachel and her group carried out a state of the art proposal motor that dissected past ways of behaving and organized customized item ideas for every client. The effect was quick and significant. Clients felt seen, comprehended, and esteemed - changing the conditional into a profoundly private encounter.

As she encountered doubters who questioned the viability of such a radical shift, Rachel's resilience was put to the test. Determined, she remained convinced that personalization was a showcasing strategy as well as a way of thinking that put the client at the core of the brand.

The innovation pioneered by Rachel had reverberated throughout the sector. Contenders mixed to get up to speed, yet Rachel had set another norm for client driven advertising. The landscape of e-commerce transformed into a dynamic market where brands competed not only for the emotional connection they made with their customers but also for the products they sold.

Rachel's steadfast obligation to personalization stretched out past calculations and examination. She was aware that human contact was necessary for genuine connection. The brand's correspondence moved from conventional messages to bona fide discussions, with customized messages tending to clients by name and recognizing their singular inclinations.

Client criticism turned into a mother lode of bits of knowledge for Rachel. She didn't just accept criticism; rather, she actively sought it out, seeing each comment as an opportunity to improve the personalized experience. This open discourse fashioned areas of strength for a between the brand and its clients, making a local area that felt appreciated and esteemed.

A culture of ongoing improvement was fueled by Rachel's tenacity that got her through the difficulties of implementation. The showcasing group turned into a powerful power, continually emphasizing and developing to remain on the ball. In group gatherings, Rachel underlined the significance of flexibility and gaining from the two triumphs and disappointments.

The effect of Rachel's inventive methodology stretched out past the advanced domain. The brand's obligation to personalization rose above web-based communications, flawlessly coordinating with in-store encounters. Clients strolled into actual stores welcomed by educated staff who were equipped with bits of knowledge gathered from their web-based cooperations.

As word spread of Rachel's prosperity, industry gatherings looked for her as a featured subject matter expert. Her story turned into a reference point of motivation for advertisers exploring the perplexing scene of the computerized age. Rachel's process wasn't just about changing advertising; it was a demonstration of the force of strength, development, and a certified association with clients.

In the end, Rachel Brooks did more than just tell a story about marketing personalization; she created a story of change, flexibility, and a promise to grasping the heartbeat of the client. Her story serves as a reminder that in the ever-evolving business world, people who are willing to change can create a future in which personalized experiences are not just a strategy but a real way to show empathy and connection.

Definition of Personalization in Marketing

Personalization in showcasing alludes to the act of fitting advertising messages, items, and encounters to meet the singular necessities and inclinations of buyers. It entails using technology and data to create individualized interactions that resonate with particular audiences and ultimately increase customer satisfaction and engagement.

At its center, personalization is tied in with perceiving that not all clients are something similar. It recognizes the variety in inclinations, ways of behaving, and socioeconomics among customers and looks to convey a more important and significant experience to every person. This approach diverges from conventional mass showcasing, where nonexclusive messages are communicated to an expansive crowd in the desire for catching consideration.

One critical component of personalization is information. Organizations gather and dissect tremendous measures of information to comprehend their clients better. This information can incorporate buy history, online way of behaving, segment data, and even inclinations communicated by the client. Businesses can use this data to create detailed customer profiles, allowing them to better target their marketing efforts.

Personalization stretches out past basically tending to clients by their names in messages. It envelops a scope of systems and innovations pointed toward giving a special encounter to every buyer. For example, internet business stages frequently use calculations to suggest items in view of a client's perusing and buy history. By presenting items that are compatible with the individual's interests, this not only makes the shopping experience more convenient but also increases the likelihood of a purchase.

Personalization is evident across a variety of marketing channels in addition to product recommendations. Site personalization, for instance, includes changing the substance and design of a site in view of a client's inclinations or conduct. This can incorporate displaying applicable substance, proposing related items, or modifying the UI to upgrade route.

Personalization is another important aspect of email marketing. Past utilizing the beneficiary's name, customized messages can incorporate custom-made item proposals, select offers in view of past buys, and content that lines up with the beneficiary's advantages. The objective is to make the correspondence seriously convincing and applicable, expanding the possibilities of transformation.

Personalization is also being used by social media platforms to make the user experience better. To create personalized feeds, algorithms on platforms like Facebook and Instagram look at user engagement and preferences. Sponsors, thus, can target explicit socioeconomics with redid content, guaranteeing their messages contact the most pertinent crowds.

The ascent of computerized reasoning (simulated intelligence) and AI has fundamentally progressed the capacities of personalization in showcasing. These innovations empower organizations to mechanize the examination of tremendous datasets, distinguish designs, and anticipate individual inclinations. Chatbots controlled by computer based intelligence, for instance, can draw in with clients continuously, giving customized suggestions or help in light of client input.

Personalization in marketing raises ethical issues, particularly with regard to data privacy, despite the obvious benefits. There is a delicate balance between personalization and intrusion as businesses collect and use personal information to tailor experiences. Finding the right balance is essential for establishing and maintaining customer trust. Straightforwardness in information works on, getting assent, and guaranteeing strong safety efforts are fundamental parts of a moral way to deal with personalization.

Furthermore, a thorough comprehension of the intended audience is essential for successful personalization. Organizations should put resources into statistical surveying and ceaselessly update their client profiles to remain applicable. Neglecting to adjust to changing inclinations or neglecting to precisely decipher information can bring about off track personalization endeavors, possibly distancing clients instead of connecting with them.

In conclusion, personalization in marketing is a dynamic and transformative strategy that aims to create one-of-a-kind and individualized customer experiences. Filled by information, innovation, and man-made brainpower, personalization goes past tending to clients by name and envelops a large number of procedures across different promoting channels. While it improves client commitment and fulfillment, moral contemplations and a profound comprehension of the ideal interest group are essential for its fruitful execution. As innovation keeps on advancing, personalization is probably going to assume a considerably more basic part in molding the eventual fate of showcasing.

Importance of Tailored Customer Experiences

Custom-made client encounters have become vital in the contemporary business scene, reshaping the manner in which organizations communicate with their customer base. In this present reality where rivalry is wild and purchaser assumptions are developing quickly, the meaning of giving customized cooperations couldn't possibly be more significant. This approach rises above simple consumer loyalty; it is tied in with laying out significant associations, encouraging reliability, and eventually driving business achievement.

One of the essential justifications for why custom-made client encounters matter lies in the extraordinary inclinations and necessities of individual clients. Customers no longer want generic, one-size-fits-all solutions; they want individualized interactions that reflect their particular interests and needs. A customized approach recognizes the variety among clients, perceiving that every individual is unmistakable and values an exceptional arrangement of characteristics in the items or administrations they look for.

Personalization stretches out past just tending to clients by their names; it includes figuring out their inclinations, buy history, and conduct. Furnished with this information, organizations can create designated showcasing messages, suggest applicable items, and smooth out the general client venture. Thus, organizations exhibit a certifiable obligation to meeting the particular requirements of their clients, upgrading their general fulfillment and improving the probability of rehash business.

In addition, fitted client encounters contribute altogether to the client unwaveringly. In a period where purchasers have an overflow of decisions, brand reliability is a valuable item. Clients are bound to stay faithful to a brand that addresses their issues as well as goes above and beyond to cause them to feel esteemed and comprehended. Customized corporations make a close to home association, encouraging a feeling of dedication that rises above value-based connections.

Take for instance a scenario in which an e-commerce platform makes product recommendations based on a customer's browsing and previous purchases. This customized approach makes the shopping experience more helpful as well as develops a sensation of being perceived and taken care of. Thus, clients are more disposed to pick that stage for future buys, framing a drawn out relationship that reaches out past a solitary exchange.

Moreover, fitted client encounters add to expanded consumer loyalty and positive informal exchange advertising. Fulfilled clients are bound to impart their positive encounters to other people, whether through web-based entertainment, online surveys, or informal. In a computerized age where data ventures quickly, positive surveys and suggestions can fundamentally affect a brand's standing and draw in new clients.

On the other hand, inability to give customized encounters can prompt disappointment and estrangement. Clients might feel like simply one more number in an ocean of exchanges, reducing their association with the brand. Negative encounters are likewise bound to be shared, possibly hurting the organization's standing. Subsequently, putting resources into custom-made client encounters isn't just about gathering current client assumptions yet in addition shielding the brand's picture and drawing in new clients through sure surveys and tributes.

As well as upgrading client unwaveringly and fulfillment, customized encounters add to further developed client maintenance. Holding existing clients is many times more practical than getting new ones. At the point when clients feel esteemed and comprehended, they are more averse to investigate elective choices. This lessens client stir as well as gives a steady client base, making an establishment for supported business development.

Custom-made client encounters are especially pertinent in the computerized age, where information examination and man-made consciousness assume a crucial part. Through cutting edge examination, organizations can assemble significant experiences into client conduct, inclinations, and patterns. Companies can anticipate customer requirements, personalize offerings, and develop targeted marketing strategies by making use of this data.

A streaming service might, for instance, recommend content based on a user's previous viewing habits. This not only makes the user experience better but also makes it more likely that the customer will keep using the service. The capacity to outfit information for personalization engages organizations to remain in front of market drifts and furnish creative arrangements that line up with developing client inclinations.

All in all, the significance of custom-made client encounters couldn't possibly be more significant in the present serious business scene. Personalization is more than just a fad; it is an essential basis for organizations hoping to flourish in a client driven climate. By getting it and answering the extraordinary necessities of individual clients, organizations can encourage dedication, drive consumer loyalty, and position themselves for supported achievement. In a period where clients look for something other than items or administrations - they look for significant associations - fitted encounters are the way to opening long haul connections and business development.

Chapter 1
Evolution of
Personalizatio

n and Historical Overview

The development of personalization in different parts of our lives has been a unique excursion, molded by mechanical headways, social moves, and changing buyer assumptions. This verifiable outline follows the direction of personalization from its unassuming starting points to the complex, information driven frameworks we experience today.

In the good 'ol days, personalization was a manual and restricted process. Think back to the neighborhood corner store where the proprietor knew every customer by name, their preferences, and even the members of their families. This customized administration was based on direct connections and a profound comprehension of individual necessities. As social orders developed, this degree of personalization became testing to keep up with.

The coming of broad communications and showcasing in the twentieth century denoted a critical shift. Organizations embraced a more transmission situated approach, contacting enormous crowds with normalized messages. Be that as it may, this approach coming up short on subtlety of personalization. It regarded purchasers as an aggregate as opposed to perceiving their interesting personalities and inclinations.

The ascent of the web in the late twentieth century achieved a change in outlook. Personalization began to mesh its direction into online encounters. Early sites permitted clients to tweak their points of interaction or set inclinations, yet these were much of the time restricted to essential decisions.

Email administrations started customizing inboxes in light of client conduct, and online business stages suggested items in view of procurement history.

The 21st century saw a blast of personalization filled by information. Web-based entertainment stages became instrumental in gathering immense measures of client information, empowering designated publicizing and content suggestions. Calculations began investigating client conduct, anticipating inclinations, and fitting encounters across different computerized stages.

The development of personalization also spread to the entertainment industry. Real time features like Netflix altered how we consume content by presenting customized proposals. Their calculations think about survey history, type inclinations, and, surprisingly, the hour of day to propose content custom-made to individual preferences.

The portable insurgency further escalated personalization. Smartphones became effective instruments for data collection, and apps began providing highly individualized experiences. Customized warnings, area based administrations, and relevant suggestions became essential to the versatile client experience.

Internet business stages refined their personalization techniques, utilizing AI calculations to figure out client conduct and convey customized item suggestions. Online retailers began utilizing customized messages, dynamic evaluating, and designated advancements to improve client commitment and increment transformation rates.

In the domain of medical services, personalization has advanced to work on quiet results. Electronic wellbeing records empower customized treatment plans in light of individual well being information. Users' activity is tracked and analyzed by wearable devices and health apps, which provides individualized insights and encourages healthier lifestyles.

Schooling has not been resistant to the flood of personalization. Educational content is tailored to each student's needs, pacing, and learning styles with adaptive learning platforms. This approach plans to expand learning productivity and take special care of assorted abilities to learn.

As personalization turned out to be more refined, worries about protection and information security arose. The rising dependence on private information to fuel calculations brought up moral issues about the mindful utilization of data. To protect user privacy, governments and regulatory bodies responded with data protection laws and regulations.

The eventual fate of personalization is probably going to be molded by headways in man-made consciousness (simulated intelligence) and AI.

These advancements can possibly examine huge datasets at extraordinary velocities, further refining customized encounters. Menial helpers controlled by computer based intelligence might turn out to be significantly more capable at understanding and expecting client needs.

All in all, the development of personalization is an entrancing excursion that mirrors our changing relationship with innovation. Personalization has come a long way, from the intimate interactions of a local shopkeeper to the data-driven algorithms of today. It has changed the manner in which we shop, consume content, get medical care, and learn. While the advantages are obvious, finding some kind of harmony among personalization and security will be an urgent test in the continuous story of this powerful development.

Technological Advancements Shaping Personalization

Mechanical headways have upset how personalization is incorporated into different parts of our lives. Technology has been a major factor in shaping and improving personalization in a variety of ways, including personalized recommendations on streaming platforms and shopping experiences. This advancement is driven by the rising abilities of computerized reasoning (man-made intelligence), AI (ML), and information investigation.

One huge region where mechanical progressions have significantly affected personalization is in the domain of diversion. Advanced algorithms are used by streaming services like Netflix, Spotify, and Amazon Prime Video to study user preferences and actions. These stages use AI to prescribe content custom fitted to individual preferences, making an exceptionally customized review or listening experience. As clients interface with the stage, the calculations ceaselessly learn and adjust, refining their ideas in light of the client's advancing inclinations.

Web based business has likewise seen a groundbreaking change in personalization because of mechanical progressions. Online retailers utilize complex calculations to investigate client conduct, buy history, and inclinations. This information is then used to give customized item suggestions, designated commercials, and, surprisingly, tweaked valuing. For example, on the off chance that a client habitually looks for running shoes, an internet business stage might focus on showing sports and wellness related items during their visit.

Besides, headways in expanded reality (AR) and computer generated reality (VR) advancements add to a more vivid and customized web based shopping experience. Clients can practically take a stab at dress, envision furniture in their homes, or even test cosmetics items through AR applications. This improves the personalization perspective as well as lessens the vulnerability related with online buys, prompting expanded consumer loyalty.

The wave of technological advancements that are influencing personalization has not gone unnoticed in the healthcare sector. Wearable gadgets and wellbeing applications gather continuous information on people's exercises, rest designs, and important bodily functions.

Healthcare providers are able to provide tailored wellness recommendations and interventions thanks to this information. Patients can get custom-made guidance in view of their special wellbeing information, encouraging a proactive way to deal with medical care.

In schooling, customized learning stages influence computer based intelligence to adjust to individual understudies' necessities and learning styles. These stages examine understudies' presentation, distinguish solid areas and shortcoming, and progressively change the educational program to suit their speed and inclinations. This approach expands the effectiveness of getting the hang of, taking special care of the different necessities of understudies and advancing a really captivating instructive experience.

The auto business has seen huge headways in personalization through shrewd vehicle advances. Associated vehicles outfitted with IoT (Web of Things) gadgets can gain proficiency with drivers' propensities, inclinations, and driving styles. By adapting to the individual preferences of each user, these vehicles enhance the driving experience by recommending preferred routes and adjusting seat positions.

Customized promoting has gone through an insurgency with the coming of innovation. Marketers are able to create highly targeted and personalized campaigns through the use of AI-driven tools and big data analytics.

By investigating client conduct and socioeconomics, advertisers can convey custom fitted substance, offers, and promotions to explicit crowd fragments. This works on the adequacy of advertising endeavors as well as improves the general client experience.

Web-based entertainment stages are another space where innovative progressions have essentially impacted personalization. To curate personalized feeds, algorithms on platforms like Facebook, Instagram, and Twitter look at user interactions, content preferences, and engagement patterns. Users are kept engaged by this personalized content delivery, which encourages continued use of these platforms.

In the domain of shrewd homes, the Web of Things (IoT) plays had a focal impact in customizing the residing experience. Brilliant home gadgets can learn client propensities and inclinations, changing lighting, temperature, and different settings as needs be. Controlling these smart devices through voice-activated virtual assistants like Google Assistant and Amazon's Alexa creates a streamlined and individualized home environment.

In any case, as innovation keeps on propelling, worries about information protection and security become more noticeable. Questions about how this information is handled and protected arise from the extensive collection and use of personal data for personalization purposes.

Finding some kind of harmony between giving customized encounters and defending client protection stays a basic test that both innovation engineers and policymakers should address.

All in all, mechanical headways have introduced another time of personalization across different spaces of our lives. From amusement and internet business to medical care and schooling, the reconciliation of artificial intelligence, AI, and information examination has considered exceptionally custom fitted and vivid encounters. While these progressions bring various advantages, the moral contemplations encompassing protection and information security highlight the requirement for mindful turn of events and execution of customized technology.

Chapter 2
Benefits of Personalizatio n in Marketing

The way businesses connect with their audience is being transformed by the numerous advantages of personalization in marketing. This customized approach upgrades client encounters, encourages brand unwaveringly, and drives commitment. Here is a top to bottom investigation of the vital benefits of integrating personalization into your promoting systems.

Improved Client Experience:

Personalization empowers organizations to convey content and messages customized to individual inclinations, ways of behaving, and socioeconomics. By understanding clients on a more profound level, organizations can make a more charming and important experience. This not only makes customers feel like they are understood, but it also makes them happier, which makes people think well of the brand.

Expanded Client Commitment:

Customized content reverberates more with the crowd, catching their consideration and empowering communication. Whether it's customized messages, item suggestions, or designated ads, clients are bound to draw in with content that straightforwardly addresses their requirements and interests.

This uplifted commitment can bring about expanded navigate rates, virtual entertainment associations, and generally speaking brand mindfulness.

Increased Rates of Conversion:

At the point when clients experience customized encounters, they are bound to change over. Customized item proposals, designated offers, and redid informing can fundamentally affect the dynamic cycle. Businesses have the ability to influence consumers' purchasing decisions and increase conversion rates by providing what they need at the right time to their customers.

Further developed Client Maintenance:

Personalization encourages a feeling of steadfastness and association between the client and the brand. At the point when people feel that a brand comprehends their inclinations and takes special care of their necessities, they are bound to stay steadfast clients. In today's competitive market, personalization plays a crucial role in retaining customers, and repeat business is essential for long-term success.

Information Driven Bits of knowledge:

Personalization depends vigorously on information investigation. By gathering and investigating client information, organizations gain important bits of knowledge into client conduct, inclinations, and patterns. These bits of knowledge can illuminate key choices, permitting organizations to refine their showcasing endeavors and better meet the advancing requirements of their crowd.

Expanded Client Lifetime Worth:

As personalization improves client faithfulness and supports rehash business, it adds to an expansion in client lifetime esteem. At the point when clients reliably have positive encounters with a brand, they are bound to make extra buys and become advocates, driving long haul benefits for the business.

Advanced Advertising return for money invested:

Businesses can better allocate their marketing resources with personalization. By focusing on unambiguous portions with customized crusades, organizations can upgrade their profit from venture (return for money invested).

This accuracy guarantees that showcasing financial plans are spent on drives that are bound to yield positive outcomes.

Reinforced Brand Picture:

A brand's value and comprehension of its customers are demonstrated by a personalized approach. In turn, this helps build a good reputation for the brand. Clients are bound to trust and support marks that try to customize their corporations. Positive brand insight can prompt natural informal exchange showcasing, further growing the brand's range.

Strategically pitching and Upselling Open doors:

Customized suggestions in view of client conduct and inclinations open up doors for strategically pitching and upselling. By recommending integral items or premium overhauls that line up with individual inclinations, organizations can expand the typical exchange esteem and amplify income per client.

Transformation to Changing Buyer Assumptions:

In the computerized age, shoppers anticipate customized encounters. Organizations that embrace personalization exhibit their obligation to living up to these assumptions, remaining pertinent in a quickly developing business sector. Neglecting to integrate personalization might prompt a distinction with buyers who have generally expected custom-made connections.

All in all, the advantages of personalization in advertising are broad and significant. From upgrading client encounters and commitment to enhancing showcasing return for capital invested and reinforcing brand devotion, personalization is a useful asset for current organizations. As innovation keeps on propelling, the capacity to bridle information for customized advertising will turn out to be much more basic for remaining serious and cultivating enduring associations with clients.

Enhanced Customer Engagement

Improved client commitment is a significant part of present day business techniques, incorporating a complex way to deal with interface with clients on a more profound level. In the present cutthroat scene, where items and administrations frequently share comparable highlights and functionalities, organizations are progressively understanding the meaning of cultivating significant associations with their client base.

At the center of upgraded client commitment is the comprehension that clients are not just value-based elements yet rather people with remarkable inclinations, necessities, and assumptions. Businesses have adopted a holistic strategy that places an emphasis on customer satisfaction, loyalty, and advocacy as a result of this paradigm shift.

One of the vital components of improved client commitment is customized correspondence. Utilizing information investigation and computerized reasoning, organizations can assemble bits of knowledge into client conduct, inclinations, and buy history. Furnished with this data, organizations can tailor their correspondence methodologies, conveying designated and significant substance to individual clients. Whether through customized messages, suggestions, or elite offers, organizations can make a more custom-made and significant connection, reverberating with clients on an individual level.

In addition, the ascent of virtual entertainment stages has changed the manner in which organizations draw in with their clients. Web-based entertainment gives a dynamic and intuitive channel for correspondence, empowering organizations to communicate their messages as well as to tune in and answer client criticism effectively.

Convenient and straightforward correspondence via web-based entertainment stages fabricates trust and encourages a feeling of local area, as clients feel appreciated and esteemed.

Notwithstanding customized correspondence, organizations are progressively putting resources into intelligent encounters to upgrade client commitment. Computer generated reality (VR) and expanded reality (AR) advances have opened up new roads for vivid and noteworthy collaborations.

For instance, furniture retailers can offer virtual display areas, permitting clients to envision items in their own living spaces prior to making a buy. Such intuitive encounters separate a brand as well as make an enduring impression, fortifying the profound association between the client and the brand.

Besides, the execution of chatbots and menial helpers has reformed client service, giving moment and nonstop help. These insightful frameworks can deal with routine questions, guide clients through investigating cycles, and, surprisingly, give item suggestions in view of individual inclinations. Via computerizing these cycles, organizations further develop proficiency as well as let loose HR to zero in on more complicated and high-esteem corporations.

Upgraded client commitment is certainly not a one-time exertion however a continuous obligation to understanding and adjusting to developing client needs. Client criticism systems, for example, studies and surveys, assume a pivotal part in this consistent improvement process.

By effectively looking for and answering client criticism, organizations exhibit a guarantee to consumer loyalty and an eagerness to develop in light of client bits of knowledge.

In addition, dedication projects and client rewards are viable devices for upgrading commitment and cultivating brand faithfulness. These projects go past simple limits, offering clients elite admittance to occasions, early item dispatches, or customized advantages.

Businesses can cultivate long-term relationships that go beyond individual transactions by making customers feel like they are valued members of a community.

All in all, upgraded client commitment is an essential basic for organizations exploring the intricacies of the cutting edge commercial center. By embracing customized correspondence, intelligent encounters, Innovation driven arrangements, and a guarantee to client criticism, organizations can have serious areas of strength for producing enduring associations with their client base.

In a period where client unwaveringly is a valuable product, the interest in upgraded client commitment isn't just an upper hand however a foundation of economical business achievement.

Increased Customer Loyalty

Expanded client reliability is a significant consideration for the outcome of any business. Building a dependable client base guarantees a steady income stream as well as adds to long haul manageability and development. Organizations that focus on and put resources into developing client reliability frequently end up in an ideal position contrasted with their rivals.

One of the essential advantages of expanded client steadfastness is the potential for higher income. Faithful clients will generally make rehash buys, and their lifetime worth to a business is fundamentally higher than that of one-time purchasers. By zeroing in on consumer loyalty and making positive encounters, organizations can encourage reliability, prompting more regular and bigger exchanges. Moreover, steadfast clients are bound to investigate and buy new items or administrations presented by a confided in brand, further adding to income development.

In addition, devoted clients frequently become brand advocates. Fulfilled clients are bound to prescribe an item or administration to companions, family, and partners. In the period of virtual entertainment and online surveys, positive verbal exchange can significantly affect an organization's standing and reach. Building a local area of faithful clients who effectively advance a brand can bring about a strong promoting force that is both practical and credible.

Client maintenance is one more pivotal viewpoint connected to expanded devotion. Securing new clients can be more costly and tedious than holding existing ones. Steadfast clients are more averse to being influenced by contenders, lessening the requirement for broad showcasing endeavors to draw in new business. Businesses can establish a solid foundation for customer retention, ultimately leading to sustained success, by consistently delivering high-quality goods or services, promptly addressing concerns, and providing excellent customer service.

A vital part of cultivating client faithfulness is making a customized and important client experience. Organizations that put resources into figuring out their clients' inclinations, ways of behaving, and needs can tailor their contributions and collaborations in like manner. Personalization goes past tending to clients by their names; it includes expecting their necessities and giving important suggestions. This degree of customization upgrades consumer loyalty as well as reinforces the close to home association between the client and the brand.

In the computerized age, innovation assumes a fundamental part in improving client unwaveringly. Client relationship the board (CRM) frameworks, information investigation, and man-made consciousness can be used to accumulate experiences into client conduct and inclinations. This information driven approach permits organizations to make designated advertising efforts, customized advancements, and dedication programs that resound with their client base. Innovation likewise empowers consistent correspondence, guaranteeing that organizations stay associated with their clients through different channels, fabricating a feeling of trust and unwavering quality.

Executing a vigorous faithfulness program is a demonstrated methodology to help client devotion. These projects, whether as focuses, limits, or restrictive advantages, boost rehash business and make a feeling of having a place among clients. In addition to rewarding customers for their loyalty, a well-designed loyalty program encourages them to engage more with the brand. It fills in as an unmistakable showing of an organization's obligation to its clients, building up the connection between the two.

Straightforwardness and genuineness are fundamental components in building and keeping up with client steadfastness. In a time where data is promptly accessible, clients esteem legitimacy. Organizations that impart straightforwardly, concede botches, and effectively look for input construct entrust with their clients. Trust is the underpinning of any enduring relationship, and when clients trust a brand, they are bound to stay faithful, even notwithstanding infrequent hiccups.

All in all, expanded client steadfastness is a multi-layered resource that contributes essentially to a business' prosperity. From supporting income and client maintenance to making brand backers and encouraging customized encounters, the advantages of focusing on client unwaveringly are various. Businesses that invest in establishing strong, long-lasting relationships with their customers are better positioned for sustained growth and prosperity in a competitive market.

Improved Conversion Rates

Businesses that want to maximize their online presence and generate revenue need to focus on raising conversion rates. A high change rate shows that a critical extent of site guests make the ideal move, whether it's making a buy, pursuing a bulletin, or finishing up a structure. Accomplishing further developed transformation rates includes an essential methodology that incorporates different components of a site, showcasing endeavors, and client experience.

One major part of helping change rates is advancing the web composition's usefulness. An easy to use communication with a natural route can essentially influence a guest's excursion. Clear and convincing suggestions to take action (CTAs) decisively positioned all through the site guide clients towards the ideal activities. Moreover, limiting interruptions and smoothing out the checkout interaction for internet business sites can assist with decreasing erosion and improve the general client experience, eventually prompting higher change rates.

Understanding the main interest group is vital in enhancing transformation rates. Analyzing user behavior data and conducting thorough market research can provide useful insights into customer preferences and issues. Fitting the site content and plan to line up with the requirements and assumptions for the interest group improves importance and commitment, improving the probability of transformations.

Powerful openness is of the utmost importance for catching and keeping a guest's advantage. Creating convincing and enticing duplicates that feature the novel incentives of items or administrations can fundamentally impact change rates. Furthermore, consolidating client tributes, surveys, and trust signals helps fabricate validity and impart trust in possible clients, tending to any reservations they might have.

Promoting targeted traffic and increasing conversion rates require the use of a robust and customized marketing strategy. Utilizing information driven experiences to make designated crusades permits organizations to contact the right crowd with the ideal message brilliantly. Using devices, for example, email showcasing, web-based entertainment promoting, and site design improvement (Web optimization) can really drive mindfulness and commitment, improving the probability of transformations.

A responsive and dynamic site is fundamental in the present computerized scene. With a developing number of clients getting to sites from cell phones, guaranteeing a consistent encounter across different screen sizes is pivotal. Versatile streamlining further develops client fulfillment as well as decidedly influences web search tool rankings, adding to expanded perceivability and possible changes.

The force of A/B testing ought to be considered carefully while looking to further develop change rates. Testing various varieties of components like titles, pictures, CTAs, and by and large formats permits organizations to distinguish what resounds most with their crowd. Ceaseless testing and advancement in view of execution information empower iterative upgrades, prompting higher transformation rates after some time.

Building entrust with guests is a basic consideration of change rate streamlining. A sense of trust is cultivated when transparent information about products or services, security certifications, and privacy policies are clearly displayed. The likelihood of a business's potential customers becoming customers is increased by making available options for customer support and promptly addressing questions or concerns.

Continuous examination and following devices assume a crucial part in checking and figuring out client conduct. By examining measurements, for example, skip rates, time nearby, and client ventures, organizations can recognize regions for development and design their techniques likewise. Using heatmaps and client meeting accounts offers significant visual bits of knowledge into how guests connect with the site, empowering organizations to upgrade explicit components for the most extreme effect on change rates.

All in all, accomplishing further developed change rates includes a comprehensive methodology that envelops web composition, client experience, designated promoting, and nonstop enhancement in light of information driven bits of knowledge. By figuring out the ideal interest group, executing viable correspondence techniques, and utilizing innovation and examination, organizations can establish a climate helpful for higher transformation rates, at last driving progress in the serious web-based scene.

Chapter 3
Key Components of Personalization

Personalization is a complex methodology that designers encounter, items, or administrations to individual inclinations and necessities. Businesses in a variety of industries are increasingly recognizing the significance of personalization to enhancing customer satisfaction, loyalty, and overall success in today's dynamic and competitive environment. To accomplish viable personalization, a few key parts assume urgent parts, molding a custom fitted and drawing in experience for every client.

1. Information Assortment and Investigation:

At the core of personalization lies information - the natural substance that fills custom fitted encounters. Hearty information assortment instruments, including client communications, inclinations, and ways of behaving, structure the establishment for personalization. After that, this data is looked at to get useful insights that help figure out what each person needs, figure out what they'll do in the future, and make a complete user profile.

2. Man-made consciousness and AI:

The sheer volume of information engaged with personalization makes it infeasible for manual investigation. Algorithms for artificial intelligence (AI) and machine learning (ML) are necessary for automating data processing. These advancements can filter through tremendous datasets, distinguish examples, and make forecasts about client inclinations, working with continuous personalization. AI and ML give businesses the ability to provide content and suggestions that are tailored to each customer, from recommendation engines to predictive analytics.

3. Client Division:

Division includes arranging clients into unmistakable gatherings in light of shared qualities or ways of behaving. By understanding these portions, organizations can fit their contributions to all the more likely meet the particular requirements of each gathering. Whether it's age, area, buy history, or commitment designs, client division takes into consideration designated personalization procedures that reverberate with the exceptional inclinations of various client portions.

4. Customized Content:

Fitting substance to individual inclinations is a foundation of personalization. This stretches out past just tending to clients by their most memorable name; delivering content that is in line with their interests, actions, and context is necessary. Product recommendations, targeted marketing messages, and dynamically adjusting website interfaces based on user preferences are all examples of personalized content. Content personalization encourages a more profound association between the client and the brand, upgrading commitment and fulfillment.

5. Dynamic UIs:

Static sites and applications are advancing into dynamic conditions that adjust to individual clients progressively. Dynamic UIs change design, content, and highlights in view of client conduct and inclinations. This degree of personalization guarantees that every client has a one of a kind and streamlined insight, further developing convenience and by and large fulfillment.

6. Omnichannel Personalization:

As clients communicate with brands across different channels - from sites and portable applications to virtual entertainment and in-store encounters - a consistent and predictable personalization procedure is vital. Omnichannel personalization guarantees that client inclinations and collaborations are synchronized across all touchpoints, making a firm and coordinated insight. In addition to increasing user satisfaction, this helps to create a unified brand image.

7. Management of Consent and Privacy:

In the time of information security concerns, straightforwardness and client assent are basic parts of compelling personalization. Organizations should lay out trust by plainly conveying their information utilization rehearses and getting express assent from clients. Security upgrading innovations and vigorous assent of the executives' frameworks assist with finding some kind of harmony among personalization and defending client protection.

8. Continuous Improvement:

The process of personalization is iterative and requires constant improvement and optimization. Dissecting client input, observing execution measurements, and adjusting personalization methodologies in light of advancing client ways of behaving are fundamental. Personalization efforts remain successful and in line with shifting user expectations and market trends thanks to continuous optimization.

All in all, fruitful personalization is an amicable mix of information driven bits of knowledge, trend setting innovations, and a profound comprehension of client inclinations. By integrating these critical parts into their techniques, organizations can make customized encounters that reverberate with clients, encourage faithfulness, and drive supported progress in an undeniably aggressive scene.

Data Collection and Analysis

Information assortment and examination assume critical parts in different fields, going from logical exploration to business direction. The cycle includes gathering data and changing it into significant experiences, driving informed ends and activities.

Information Assortment:

1. Techniques for Information Assortment:

Information assortment strategies shift in view of the idea of the review or goal.Normal strategies incorporate reviews, meetings, perceptions, and examinations.Interviews provide qualitative information that is more in-depth, while surveys make it easy to efficiently collect large datasets. Perceptions give first hand bits of knowledge, and investigations assist with laying out causation by controlling factors.

2. Challenges in Information Assortment:

Regardless of headways in innovation, challenges endure in information assortment. The quality of the data can be impacted by bias, non-response, and incorrect responses. To mitigate these issues, it is essential to use appropriate validation methods and ensure a representative sample.

3. Innovation's Effect on Information Assortment:

Innovation has altered information assortment, robotizing processes and upgrading exactness. Versatile applications, sensors, and online structures smooth out information gathering. Web of Things (IoT) gadgets contribute constant information, offering a powerful point of view for examination.

Information Investigation:

1. Spellbinding Examination:

Elucidating examination includes summing up and introducing information in a significant manner. Measures like mean, middle, and mode give focal propensities, while standard deviation checks information scattering. Representations, like outlines and diagrams, help in passing on complex data naturally.

2. Inferential Examination:

Inferential examination digs further, reaching determinations and making forecasts past the gathered information. Factual strategies, similar to relapse investigation and speculation testing, assist with deriving connections among factors and survey the likelihood of results.

3. AI and Prescient Investigation:

Headways in AI have introduced prescient examination, permitting frameworks to gain designs from authentic information and make forecasts about future patterns. This is especially important in fields like money, medical care, and promoting.

The Exchange between Information Assortment and Investigation:

1. Iterative Interaction:

Information assortment and investigation structure an iterative interaction. Beginning information experiences might prompt changes in the assortment technique. On the other hand, unforeseen discoveries during investigation can incite returning to information hotspots for extra data.

2. Significance of Value Information:

The dependability of examination relies on the nature of gathered information. Thorough approval processes, scrupulousness during assortment, and addressing predispositions add to reliable bits of knowledge. Trash in, trash out stays a preventative guideline in the realm of information examination.

3. Moral Contemplations:

Information assortment and examination raise moral worries, particularly in the time of enormous information. Protection, assent, and dependable information use are fundamental. Finding some kind of harmony between separating significant bits of knowledge and regarding people's protection is critical to keep up with public trust.

Applications in a Variety of Branches:

1. Healthcare:

In medical services, information assortment illuminates determination, therapy plans, and general wellbeing procedures. Electronic wellbeing records, wearable gadgets, and clinical imaging contribute tremendous measures of information for investigation, working with customized medication and prescient examination.

2. Business and Promoting:

Organizations influence information to grasp buyer conduct, upgrade tasks, and settle on essential choices. Statistical surveying, client reviews, and deals information help in fitting items and administrations to satisfy developing needs.

3. Logical Exploration:

Logical revelations frequently depend on thorough information assortment and investigation. Fields like cosmology, hereditary qualities, and ecological science use advanced methods to decipher gigantic datasets, opening new bits of knowledge into the normal world.

Future Patterns:

1. Man-made reasoning Combination:

The combination of man-made brainpower (computer based intelligence) in information examination is a thriving pattern. Simulated intelligence calculations can deal with huge datasets, distinguish complex examples, and make expectations at a scale and speed unreachable by conventional strategies.

2. Moral artificial intelligence and Inclination Moderation:

As simulated intelligence assumes a bigger part in information examination, there is a developing accentuation on moral contemplations. Endeavors to relieve predispositions in calculations and guarantee fair and straightforward information rehearses are becoming key to the turn of events and arrangement of man-made intelligence frameworks.

3. Information Democratization:

Enabling people with admittance to their own information is building up some momentum. The goal of data democratization is to make information easier to get to, make it possible for people to understand and use data to their advantage, and make society more informed and involved.

All in all, the harmonious connection between information assortment and examination drives progress across different spaces. As innovation advances, moral contemplations become more essential, accentuating the obligation of experts to deal with information with care. The experiences got from this exchange can possibly shape arrangements, alter enterprises, and extend how we might interpret the world.

Customer Segmentation and Personalized Content Creation

Client division and customized content creation are vital procedures in present day showcasing, empowering organizations to fit their messages to explicit crowd fragments and upgrade in general client commitment. This unique couple is driven by the comprehension that a one-size-fits-all approach is presently not compelling in a different and carefully associated world.

Client Division:

At its center, client division includes partitioning an objective market into particular gatherings in light of shared qualities, ways of behaving, or socioeconomics. This division permits organizations to acquire further bits of knowledge into their clients, working with more designated and compelling advertising endeavors.

Segment division, for instance, includes ordering clients in view of elements like age, orientation, pay, and schooling. This gives a wide comprehension of who the clients are and could impact them. Conversely, conduct division centers around activities and inclinations, like buying history, online way of behaving, or item utilization designs. This approach uncovers experiences into why clients pursue explicit decisions and how they interface with a brand.

Division permits organizations to distinguish high-potential client gatherings and distribute assets decisively. For example, a design retailer might understand that their more youthful crowd is more dynamic via web-based entertainment, driving them to focus on internet showcasing efforts focusing on this segment.

Customized Content Creation:

When client sections are distinguished, the following stage is to make content that talks straightforwardly to each gathering. Customized content goes past basically tending to clients by their names; it includes fitting the whole message, symbolism, and tone to resound with the particular inclinations and requirements of a specific portion.

Item proposals in view of past buys or perusing conduct are an exemplary illustration of customized content. Online business goliaths, for example, influence calculations to investigate client history and inclinations, proposing items that line up with individual preferences. This improves the client experience as well as improves the probability of transformation.

Additionally, customized messages can essentially influence commitment. Making messages that take care of the interests and ways of behaving of a specific fragment encourages a feeling of significance and selectiveness. A movement organization, for example, could send oceanside excursion proposals to clients who have recently reserved comparable outings.

The Crossing point:

The real magic happens when customer segmentation and personalized content creation work together. Businesses can create hyper-targeted campaigns that deeply resonate with specific customer groups by combining these strategies. For instance, a wellness brand could distinguish a fragment of clients who reliably buy running stuff and utilize this data to create a mission based on long distance race preparing tips, joined by customized item proposals.

Besides, the information gathered through division can fuel the production of additional successful and customized content. Understanding the trouble spots, inspirations, and inclinations of each section permits organizations to tailor their information in a manner that talks straightforwardly to the necessities of their crowd.

Advantages and Difficulties:

The advantages of embracing client division and customized content creation are complex. Further developed consumer loyalty, expanded brand steadfastness, and higher transformation rates are among the positive results. Customers are more likely to engage with a brand and make subsequent purchases if they have the impression that the company understands and meets their specific requirements.

Notwithstanding, executing these systems accompanies its arrangement of difficulties. Overseeing and dissecting huge measures of information for division requires powerful innovation and examination abilities. Besides, guaranteeing that customized content remaining parts important and not nosy is a sensitive equilibrium. Clients value personalization, however there's a scarcely discernible difference among pertinence and saw obtrusiveness.

Innovation as an Empowering agent:

Progressions in innovation, especially man-made consciousness and AI, have upset the manner in which organizations approach client division and customized content creation. These advancements empower continuous examination of client information, taking into account dynamic and versatile division techniques. AI calculations can foresee client inclinations in view of advancing ways of behaving, guaranteeing that customized content remaining parts are new and significant.

Chatbots controlled by normal language handling give one more road to customized associations. These remote helpers can draw in with clients continuously, proposing customized suggestions or help in view of individual questions. In addition to improving the customer experience, this provides useful data for ongoing segmentation efforts.

In the period of data over-burden and limited capacity to focus, client division and customized content creation have become key devices for advertisers. Understanding the novel requirements and inclinations of different client portions permits organizations to slice through the commotion and interface with their crowd on a more private level.

As innovation keeps on propelling, the convergence of client division and customized content creation will probably advance. Organizations that embrace these procedures and adjust to the changing scene of shopper assumptions won't just get by however flourish in an undeniably cutthroat commercial center.

Chapter 4
Technologies Driving Personalizatio n

Personalization in innovation has turned into a foundation of client experience, molding how we communicate with different computerized stages. A few innovations are instrumental in driving this pattern, upgrading customization and fitting administrations to individual inclinations.

1. Computerized reasoning and AI:
At the front of personalization, computer based intelligence and AI calculations break down tremendous measures of client information to distinguish examples and inclinations. These advancements power suggestion frameworks, foreseeing what clients would like in light of their past way of behaving. Real time features, online business stages, and web-based entertainment influence these calculations to organize content, items, and ads custom-made to every client.

2. Normal Language Handling (NLP):

NLP assumes an essential part in personalization by empowering machines to comprehend and answer human language. NLP is used by chatbots, virtual assistants like Siri, Google Assistant, and others to comprehend user queries and respond appropriately. This upgrades the conversational part of innovation, making associations more customized and regular.

3. Virtual Reality (VR) and augmented reality (AR):

AR and VR advances are changing personalization in businesses like retail and gaming. In retail, AR permits clients to imagine items in their own space prior to settling on a buy choice. VR improves vivid encounters, empowering customized reproductions and conditions custom-made to individual inclinations, like virtual travel or preparing situations.

4. Web of Things (IoT):

The interconnected idea of IoT gadgets contributes essentially to personalization. Savvy homes, for example, adjust to client inclinations by learning everyday schedules and changing settings likewise. Wearable devices contribute to a more individualized approach to fitness and well-being by tracking health metrics and providing personalized insights.

5. Analytics of Big Data:

The expansion of huge information has opened new roads for personalization. By investigating gigantic datasets, organizations can acquire bits of knowledge into client conduct, inclinations, and patterns. Personalized marketing strategies, targeted advertising, and the creation of goods and services that meet the needs of customers are all fueled by this data.

6. Biometric Confirmation:

Personalized access to devices and services is made possible by biometric technologies like voice recognition, facial recognition, and fingerprint recognition. These technologies also improve security. These validation strategies give a consistent and customized client experience, supplanting customary passwords with safer and easy to use options.

7. Blockchain Innovation:

Blockchain adds to personalization by upgrading information security and protection. By choosing which data to share and with whom, users can exercise greater control over their personal information. This straightforwardness and control engage people, cultivating trust in customized administrations and exchanges.

8. Edge Processing:

Edge registering carries handling power nearer to the wellspring of information, decreasing inactivity and empowering quicker, more customized reactions. This is especially urgent in applications like constant personalization in retail, where speedy dynamic in light of client conduct is fundamental for a custom fitted shopping experience.

9. 5G Innovation:

The rollout of 5G organizations significantly affects personalization, particularly in versatile applications. Quicker and more solid availability works with ongoing associations, consistent streaming, and speedier admittance to customized content. This is especially apparent in expanded reality applications, web based gaming, and video web-based features.

10. Customized Medication and Wellbeing Tech:

Headways in innovation are altering medical services through customized medication. A tailored approach to treatment based on an individual's genetic makeup and lifestyle factors is made possible by genetic information, wearable devices, and health tracking applications. This shift towards accuracy medication guarantees more viable and custom-made medical services arrangements.

The integration of cutting-edge technologies is driving the ever-changing landscape of personalization. Computerized reasoning, AI, regular language handling, expanded and augmented reality, IoT, huge information examination, biometric verification, blockchain, edge processing, 5G innovation, and headways in medical care by and large add to an exceptionally customized computerized insight. As these innovations keep on developing, what's in store holds many additional thrilling opportunities for fitting innovation to individual inclinations and requirements.

Artificial Intelligence and Machine Learning

The fields of artificial intelligence (AI) and machine learning (ML) have changed the way marketing personalization is done, ushering in a time when personalized experiences are no longer a luxury but an expectation. This unique couple enables advertisers to dig into monstrous datasets, extricate significant bits of knowledge, and convey customized content that reverberates with individual shoppers.

One of the essential commitments of artificial intelligence and ML to personalization showcasing is the capacity to investigate huge measures of client information. Customary showcasing approaches frequently battled to process and get a handle on the sheer volume of data accessible. Nonetheless, with AI calculations, advertisers can proficiently filter through useful pieces of information, distinguishing examples and patterns that would be outside the realm of possibilities for a human to physically recognize.

This scientific ability empowers advertisers to make nitty gritty client profiles, grasping inclinations, ways of behaving, and commitment history. By taking advantage of this abundance of data, organizations can create exceptionally designated crusades, guaranteeing that their messages contact the perfect crowd at the ideal time. This degree of accuracy upgrades the viability of showcasing endeavors as well as cultivates a more customized and important client experience.

The use of artificial intelligence in personalization advertising stretches out outside only the ability to grasp client information. AI calculations can foresee future conduct in light of authentic examples, empowering advertisers to expect client necessities and inclinations. For example, an internet business stage using man-made intelligence could anticipate a client's next buy in view of their perusing history, past exchanges, and, surprisingly, outside factors like occasional patterns. This prescient ability enables advertisers to proactively tailor their contributions, improving the probability of transformation and consumer loyalty.

Suggestion motors, a conspicuous illustration of man-made intelligence driven personalization, assume an essential part in forming client encounters. These frameworks influence AI to examine client conduct and inclinations, giving customized ideas to items, administrations, or content. Stages like Netflix and Amazon have exhibited the force of proposal calculations in keeping clients connected with and driving deals. By ceaselessly refining suggestions in view of client connections, these frameworks make a criticism circle that upgrades personalization over the long haul.

Simulated intelligence driven personalization likewise stretches out to content creation. Regular Language Handling (NLP) calculations empower the age of customized messages, messages, or even site content. Fitting correspondence to individual inclinations, socioeconomics, and personal conduct standards helps in building a more grounded association between the brand and the client. This degree of personalization further develops commitment as well as cultivates a feeling of realness and pertinence.

Also, simulated intelligence and ML add to the advancement of promoting efforts through ongoing investigation and independent direction. Robotized frameworks can screen crusade execution, changing boundaries like promotion arrangements, focusing on measures, and informing continuously to amplify adequacy. Marketing efforts are kept in line with changing customer preferences and market trends thanks to this dynamic adaptability.

Be that as it may, the boundless reception of man-made intelligence and ML in personalization advertising raises moral contemplations. As frameworks become more proficient at understanding and foreseeing individual ways of behaving, there is a gamble of violating protection limits. Finding some kind of harmony among personalization and security is critical to building and keeping up with entrust with purchasers. Guidelines like GDPR in Europe and comparable structures overall are characteristic of the developing significance of shielding client information.

All in all, Man-made brainpower and AI have reshaped personalization in showcasing, offering extraordinary experiences and capacities. From dissecting tremendous datasets to foreseeing client conduct and conveying custom-made proposals, man-made intelligence driven personalization improves the client experience and lifts the adequacy of showcasing efforts. Personalization, on the other hand, must be guided by ethical considerations in order to safeguard user privacy and build trust. As organizations keep on saddling the force of artificial intelligence and ML, finding this harmony will be fundamental in exploring the developing scene of customized advertising.

Data Analytics Tools

Personalization marketing relies heavily on data analytics tools, which enable businesses to enhance customer experiences and increase engagement. In a time where buyers expect custom-made corporations, understanding and it is crucial for influencing information. This article investigates the meaning of information examination devices in personalization promoting, featuring key apparatuses, benefits, and arising patterns.

Significance of Personalization in Showcasing:

Personalization has turned into a foundation of current promoting systems. Buyers are immersed with data everyday, making it trying for organizations to catch their consideration. Personalization tends to this test by conveying focus on an important substance in light of individual inclinations, ways of behaving, and socioeconomics. It creates a connection between the customer and the brand, which ultimately results in brand loyalty and conversion.

Tools for Data Analysis:

Information examination devices are instrumental in gathering, handling, and deciphering huge measures of information to extricate significant bits of knowledge. With regards to personalization promoting, these devices empower organizations to grasp client conduct, inclinations, and excursion touchpoints. By outfitting information, advertisers can make profoundly customized missions and encounters that resound with their interest group.

Key Information Examination Devices in Personalization Showcasing:

Client Relationship The executives (CRM) Frameworks:

CRM frameworks are primary devices that store and oversee client information. By incorporating CRM with different information sources, organizations gain a far reaching perspective on client corporations. This information works with customized correspondence, custom-made advancements, and powerful client division.

Platforms for Data Management (DMPs):

DMPs total and sort out information from different sources, giving a concentrated center to advertisers. This empowers the production of itemized client profiles, including on the web and disconnected ways of behaving. DMPs enable marketers to provide personalized content across all channels and devices.

AI and Prescient Investigation:

AI calculations and prescient examination gauge future client conduct in view of verifiable information. These apparatuses empower advertisers to expect client needs and customize contributions progressively. Whether suggesting items or anticipating stir, AI upgrades the personalization capacities of promoting procedures.

Web Investigation Apparatuses:

Instruments like Google Investigation give bits of knowledge into site traffic, client conduct, and commitment measurements. By examining this information, advertisers can improve site encounters, convey customized content, and track the viability of personalization endeavors.

Personalization Motors:

Devoted personalization motors use calculations to convey dynamic, individualized content to clients. These motors examine client conduct, inclinations, and context oriented information to tailor site content, item suggestions, and showcasing messages continuously.

Advantages of Information Examination in Personalization Promoting:

Improved Client Commitment:

Customized encounters reverberate with clients, expanding commitment levels. A sense of connection is created when content is tailored to preferences and behaviors, which leads to relationships with the brand that last longer.

Increased Rates of Conversion:

By conveying significant and opportune substance, organizations can improve the probability of transformations. Personalization limits grinding in the client venture, directing clients toward wanted activities with more accuracy.

Expanded Client Faithfulness:

Personalization fabricates brand steadfastness as clients feel comprehended and esteemed. Steadfastness is reinforced when clients reliably get customized suggestions, advancements, and correspondence.

Upgraded Advertising Spend:
Breaking down client information assists organizations with dispensing promoting assets all the more really. By focusing on the right crowd with customized crusades, advertisers can upgrade their spending plans and boost profit from speculation.

Trends in Personalization Marketing Based on Data Analytics

Personalization Driven by AI:
Man-made reasoning (computer based intelligence) keeps on advancing, driving more complex personalization systems. Computer based intelligence controlled instruments can investigate complex datasets, distinguish designs, and convey hyper-customized encounters at scale.

Constant Personalization:
Personalization in real time is becoming increasingly popular. Organizations are utilizing information examination apparatuses to convey dynamic substance and suggestions immediately, adjusting to clients' changing inclinations and ways of behaving.

Security First Personalization:
With expanding worries about information security, organizations are taking on straightforward and moral ways to deal with personalization. Instruments that regard client protection inclinations while conveying customized encounters are acquiring unmistakable quality.

Taking everything into account, information examination instruments are the foundation of effective personalization promoting systems. To stay ahead of the competition and provide personalized experiences that captivate and retain customers, businesses must embrace technological advancements. The blend of powerful information examination and vital personalization meets client assumptions as well as impels organizations toward supported development and achievement.

Marketing Automation Platforms

By streamlining and automating marketing processes, Marketing Automation Platforms (MAPs) have revolutionized how businesses interact with their audience. These stages enable advertisers to convey customized, designated content at scale, sustaining leads and boosting the effectiveness of promoting efforts.

A Marketing Automation Platform is, at its core, a comprehensive set of tools for automating repetitive marketing tasks, managing complex campaigns, and analyzing performance metrics. One of the key advantages is the capacity to make customized client ventures. MAPs empower advertisers to create custom-made encounters for individual leads in view of their way of behaving, inclinations, and collaborations with the brand.

One essential component of Guides is lead sustaining. Rather than assaulting leads with conventional substance, these stages permit advertisers to convey the perfect message at the ideal time. Through computerized work processes, leads progress through the deals channel, getting designated content and supporting collaborations. This customized approach increments commitment as well as constructs more grounded associations with possible clients.

Moreover, Advertising Computerization Stages work with productive lead scoring. Marketers can give priority to leads that are most likely to convert by assigning scores based on how the leads behave and how engaged they are. This guarantees that sales teams will maximize their time and resources by concentrating on high-value prospects.

Email showcasing is a foundation of promoting robotization. MAPs empower the production of complex email crusades with customized content, powerful components, and set off reactions. Robotized email work processes can be set up to send the right message in light of lead conduct, guaranteeing convenient and pertinent correspondence. Moreover, A/B testing capacities inside these stages permit advertisers to refine their email procedures for ideal execution.

Web-based entertainment reconciliation is one more eminent component of Guides. Advertisers can plan and distribute posts across numerous social stages from an incorporated dashboard. This recovers time as well as guarantees steady informing. Besides, these stages give examinations to follow the presentation of social missions, permitting advertisers to change their procedures for greatest effect.

MAPs are important for adjusting deals and promoting groups. Through lead scoring, nitty gritty examination, and CRM coordination, these stages work with consistent correspondence between divisions. Outreach groups gain bits of knowledge into lead conduct and commitment, empowering them to tailor their methodology for additional successful discussions. The outcome is a more cooperative and adjusted exertion towards accomplishing hierarchical objectives.

Information driven direction is a foundation of fruitful showcasing, and Guides give hearty examination to help it. Advertisers can follow key measurements, for example, open rates, navigate rates, change rates, and that's just the beginning. These experiences empower ceaseless advancement of missions, guaranteeing that assets are apportioned to the best systems. Furthermore, Guides frequently give visual reports and dashboards for simple understanding of information.

Personalization is a vital pattern in present day promoting, and Guides assume a significant part in accomplishing it. By utilizing information on lead conduct, inclinations, and socioeconomics, advertisers can convey profoundly customized content and encounters. From dynamic email content to site personalization, these stages empower brands to interface with their crowd on a more profound level, cultivating dependability and trust.

Showcasing Mechanization Stages are not restricted to huge undertakings. Numerous stages take care of organizations, everything being equal, offering adaptable arrangements that develop with the association. Advanced marketing capabilities become more accessible as a result of this accessibility, making it easier for small and medium-sized businesses to compete with one another.

Notwithstanding, while at the same time Advertising Computerization Stages offer enormous advantages, their execution requires cautious preparation and technique. Fruitful use includes figuring out the complexities of the stage, adjusting it to business goals, and consistently improving efforts in light of information driven experiences.

Taking everything into account, Showcasing Computerization Stages have changed the scene of advanced promoting. These apparatuses enable advertisers to robotize dreary undertakings, sustain leads actually, and convey customized encounters at scale. From lead scoring and email promoting to web-based entertainment combination and investigation, Guides offer an extensive answer for present day advertisers. As organizations keep on focusing on proficiency and personalization, the job of Promoting Mechanization Stages is probably going to stay vital in forming fruitful showcasing methodologies.

Chapter 5
Challenges
and
Consideration
s Privacy
Concerns

Offering customers individualized experiences based on their preferences, behavior, and demographic information has become increasingly common in marketing. While this strategy has the potential to boost customer satisfaction and engagement, it also raises significant privacy concerns. Adjusting the advantages of personalization with the need to safeguard people's security is an intricate test that advertisers should explore.

One of the essential difficulties related with customized showcasing is the assortment and utilization of individual information. Marketers frequently collect a lot of information about individuals, such as their browsing history, purchasing habits, and even location data, in order to provide personalized experiences. While this information can be important for working on the pertinence of showcasing messages, it represents a likely danger to protection whenever misused.

Security concerns emerge when purchasers feel that their own data is being utilized without their unequivocal assent or in manners that they didn't expect. Advertisers should be straightforward about their information assortment works on, illuminating clients about the thing data is being gathered, how it will be utilized, and giving choices to quitting. The brand's reputation and trust can be damaged if this is not done.

Another thought is the gamble of information breaks. A company's ability to exploit vulnerabilities increases with the amount of personal information it collects. All-too-oft, high-profile data breaches have resulted in the disclosure of private information, allowing for identity theft and other forms of fraud. Advertisers should put resources into strong network safety measures to safeguard the individual information they handle and console buyers that their data is secure.

Notwithstanding outside dangers, organizations should likewise address inner difficulties connected with information taking care of. Guaranteeing that workers are thoroughly prepared on protection arrangements and methodology is critical. Human mistakes, for example, unintentional information spills or ill-advised admittance, can add to protection breaks. Standard reviews and updates to security conventions can assist with relieving these dangers.

The issue of agreement is fundamental to tending to protection worries in customized showcasing. Clients ought to be able to handle how their information is utilized and to give educated consent to explicit sorts regarding personalization. Clear and straightforward assent systems, for example, pick in and quit highlights, ought to be executed to engage clients to pursue educated decisions about the utilization regarding their information.

In addition, personalization's ethical aspect should not be overlooked. Advertisers should find some kind of harmony between giving applicable substance and staying away from control. People and society as a whole can suffer as a result of personalization techniques used to exploit weaknesses or control emotions. It is essential to adhere to fairness and transparency principles and establish ethical guidelines for personalized marketing practices.

In terms of privacy, new technologies like artificial intelligence and machine learning present additional obstacles. These innovations empower more refined and nuanced personalization, however they additionally include complex calculations that may not be completely straightforward to clients. Advertisers need to guarantee that simulated intelligence driven personalization is reasonable, justifiable, and lines up with protection guidelines.

Administrative consistency is a basic thought in tending to protection worries in customized showcasing. Regulations like the Overall Information Security Guideline (GDPR) in Europe and the California Buyer Protection Act (CCPA) in the US have severe prerequisites in regards to the assortment, handling, and capacity of individual information. Organizations working in various locales should explore a mind boggling scene of guidelines, requiring an exhaustive comprehension of security regulations and a promise to be consistent.

As protection guidelines develop, advertisers should remain informed and adjust their practices appropriately. There may be severe penalties and legal consequences for noncompliance. Besides, embracing a security first methodology can be an upper hand, as purchasers progressively focus on brands that exhibit a promise to safeguard their protection.

Regardless of these difficulties, personalization stays a useful asset for advertisers when drawn nearer dependably. By zeroing in on protection by plan - coordinating security contemplations into the improvement of customized advertising methodologies - organizations can fabricate entrust with buyers and separate themselves on the lookout. This includes executing security upgrading innovations, leading protection influence appraisals, and routinely assessing and refreshing protection strategies.

Taking everything into account, the crossing point of personalization and protection presents the two valuable open doors and difficulties for advertisers. Adjusting the advantages of customized showcasing with the basics to safeguard people's protection requires a comprehensive methodology that incorporates straightforward information rehearses, hearty safety efforts, moral contemplations, and consistency with developing security guidelines. By focusing on protection and taking on mindful practices, advertisers can bridle the force of personalization while cultivating trust and reliability among their client base.

Balancing Personalization with Consumer Trust

Offsetting personalization with buyer trust is a fragile dance that cutting edge organizations should dominate in the period of information driven promoting. As organizations progressively influence client information to tailor their contributions, there is a developing need to lay out and keep up with entrust with buyers who are turning out to be more aware of protection concerns.

At the core of this challenge is the pressure between giving a customized experience that takes special care of individual inclinations and keeping up with the protection and security of purchasers' information. On the one hand, customers value personalized services for their convenience and relevance. Then again, there is a developing mindfulness and worry about how organizations gather, store, and use individual data.

One critical part of accomplishing this equilibrium is straightforwardness. Organizations that are open and clear about their information assortment rehearses are bound to procure and keep up with customer trust. Demystifying the personalization process and fostering a sense of control for customers can be accomplished by clearly communicating what data is collected, how it is used, and the security measures in place.

Besides, acquiring unequivocal assent from clients prior to gathering their information is vital. By giving customers the option to opt in or out of personalized services, this not only complies with privacy laws but also gives them more control over their own lives. An educated and willing member is bound to feel in charge of their information, reinforcing the groundwork of trust.

Finding some kind of harmony additionally includes executing strong safety efforts. Information breaks and misusing of individual data can dissolve customer trust rapidly. Organizations should put resources into state of the art network safety measures to shield the information they gather. Exhibiting a promise to safeguard client data consoles purchasers and supports that their security is a main concern.

However, ethical data use is essential even with open communication and stringent security measures. Organizations should oppose the compulsion to take advantage of individual data for momentary gains or control buyer conduct in manners that might be seen as meddlesome. A moral way to deal with information utilization includes regarding limits, staying away from superfluous intrusions of security, and guaranteeing that the advantages of personalization are shared.

Teaching purchasers about the worth of trade is one more significant component in building trust. At the point when people comprehend that giving some private data empowers organizations to offer more custom fitted and applicable administrations, they might be more ready to share such information. Organizations ought to stress the advantages purchasers get as a trade-off for sharing their data, whether it be customized proposals, selective limits, or a smoother client experience.

Additionally, ceaseless openness is absolutely vital for keeping up with trust. As organizations develop their personalization techniques, keeping clients informed about changes in information rehearses guarantees straightforwardness. Routinely refreshing protection strategies and giving roads to client criticism can exhibit a promise to transparency and responsibility.

As innovation propels, the significance of client control turns out to be considerably more articulated. Enabling purchasers to deal with their protection settings, control the degree of personalization, and effectively quit whenever wanted gives a feeling of independence. Easy to understand interfaces that enable people to modify their security inclinations add to a positive client experience and support the possibility that personalization is an instrument at the removal of the customer.

Furthermore, regarding social and provincial varieties in perspectives towards protection is fundamental. Various social orders have unmistakable points of view on private data, and a one-size-fits-all approach might prompt false impressions and disintegrate trust.

Adjusting personalization systems to line up with nearby assumptions and guidelines shows a worldwide mindfulness and a pledge to regarding different protection standards.

All in all, offsetting personalization with shopper trust is a complex test that requires a comprehensive methodology. Straightforwardness, unequivocal assent, strong safety efforts, moral information utilization, instruction, nonstop correspondence, client control, and social awareness are essential components of accomplishing this sensitive harmony. Organizations that focus on these angles not just explore the intricacies of the cutting edge information scene effectively yet additionally assemble enduring associations with buyers in light of trust and shared benefit.

Chapter 6
Successful
Case Studies

Personalization promotion has turned into a foundation of effective computerized procedures, as organizations endeavor to make more significant and pertinent cooperations with their clients. From the perspective of contextual analyses, we can gather significant bits of knowledge into the viability of personalization in driving commitment, upgrading client encounters, and at last supporting business results.

One striking contextual investigation is that of Amazon, a worldwide web based business goliath that has excelled at personalization. Amazon's proposal motor dissects client conduct, buy history, and inclinations to arrange customized item ideas. This approach altogether adds to the organization's great change rates and client maintenance. By conveying fitted substance to clients, Amazon makes a feeling of individualized consideration, encouraging devotion and rehash business.

Also, Netflix has reformed media outlets through its customized content proposals. The web-based feature investigates seeing propensities, appraisals, and, surprisingly, the hour of day clients draw in with the stage to recommend motion pictures and Television programs customized to individual inclinations. This hyper-customized approach keeps clients connected as well as assumes a critical part in lessening stir, as clients feel a more profound association with the stage.

Moving past the domains of online business and diversion, Spotify's outcome in the music streaming industry is one more demonstration of the force of personalization. By utilizing client information, including listening history and type inclinations, Spotify curates customized playlists like Find Week by week and Delivery Radar. These arranged playlists upgrade client fulfillment as well as drive client commitment and maintenance, displaying the effect of personalization in the cutthroat music streaming scene.

In the domain of online travel services, Booking.com stands apart for its customized way to deal with convenience proposals. The stage uses information on client search history, area inclinations, and past appointments to give customized inn ideas. This works on the booking system for clients as well as improves the probability of change by introducing choices lined up with individual inclinations.

The style business has additionally embraced personalization with examples of overcoming adversity, for example, Line Fix. This web based styling administration utilizes a blend of algorithmic suggestions and human beauticians to organize customized clothing determinations for clients. Line Fix's model improves the shopping experience as well as supports rehash business, as clients value the comfort and individual touch in their arranged design decisions.

One of the basic elements in the progress of these contextual analyses is the usage of man-made consciousness (simulated intelligence) and AI calculations. Businesses are able to process large amounts of data more effectively thanks to these technologies, which also allow them to accurately predict user preferences and patterns. The cooperative energy among innovation and personalization enables organizations to convey custom-made encounters at scale, driving consumer loyalty and devotion.

Past the purchaser confronting businesses, B2B organizations have likewise tackled the force of personalization. AI-driven personalization is used by Salesforce, a market leader in customer relationship management (CRM), to improve the user experience within its platform. By understanding client conduct, Salesforce tailors the point of interaction, proposes applicable elements, and furnishes bits of knowledge that line up with individual client jobs, at last expanding client reception and fulfillment.

Personalization has also changed the game when it comes to email marketing. For a situation study including clothing retailer ASOS, the execution of customized email crusades prompted a critical expansion in open rates and navigate rates. ASOS delivered targeted content that resonated with each customer segment by segmenting their audience based on preferences, purchase history, and browsing behavior. This improved engagement and conversion rates.

The outcome of these contextual analyses highlights the significance of a client driven approach in the period of computerized showcasing. Beyond simply addressing customers by their first name, personalization includes figuring out their inclinations, expecting their necessities, and conveying custom-made encounters across different touchpoints. As innovation keeps on advancing, organizations should adjust and use the capacities of artificial intelligence, AI, and information examination to remain ahead in the cutthroat scene.

Taking everything into account, the effect of fruitful contextual analyses on personalization advertising is significant and sweeping. Businesses in a variety of industries, including e-commerce giants like Amazon and Netflix and niche players like Stitch Fix, have reaped the benefits of providing personalized customer experiences. The consistent idea among these examples of overcoming adversity is the essential utilization of innovation, information examination, and a certified obligation to understanding and meeting individual client needs. Businesses that prioritize and invest in personalization will likely stand out in a crowded market as personalization continues to evolve, resulting in stronger connections with their target audience and long-term success.

Notable Examples of Effective Personalization Strategies

Personalization promotion has turned into a foundation of effective computerized procedures, as organizations endeavor to make more significant and pertinent cooperations with their clients. From the perspective of contextual analyses, we can gather significant bits of knowledge into the viability of personalization in driving commitment, upgrading client encounters, and at last supporting business results.

One striking contextual investigation is that of Amazon, a worldwide web based business goliath that has excelled at personalization. Amazon's proposal motor dissects client conduct, buy history, and inclinations to arrange customized item ideas. This approach altogether adds to the organization's great change rates and client maintenance. By conveying fitted substance to clients, Amazon makes a feeling of individualized consideration, encouraging devotion and rehash business.

Also, Netflix has reformed media outlets through its customized content proposals. The web-based feature investigates seeing propensities, appraisals, and, surprisingly, the hour of day clients draw in with the stage to recommend motion pictures and Television programs customized to individual inclinations. This hyper-customized approach keeps clients connected as well as assumes a critical part in lessening stir, as clients feel a more profound association with the stage.

Moving past the domains of online business and diversion, Spotify's outcome in the music streaming industry is one more demonstration of the force of personalization. By utilizing client information, including listening history and type inclinations, Spotify curates customized playlists like Find Week by week and Delivery Radar. These arranged playlists upgrade client fulfillment as well as drive client commitment and maintenance, displaying the effect of personalization in the cutthroat music streaming scene.

In the domain of online travel services, Booking.com stands apart for its customized way to deal with convenience proposals. The stage uses information on client search history, area inclinations, and past appointments to give customized inn ideas. This works on the booking system for clients as well as improves the probability of change by introducing choices lined up with individual inclinations.

The style business has additionally embraced personalization with examples of overcoming adversity, for example, Line Fix. This web based styling administration utilizes a blend of algorithmic suggestions and human beauticians to organize customized clothing determinations for clients. Line Fix's model improves the shopping experience as well as supports rehash business, as clients value the comfort and individual touch in their arranged design decisions.

One of the basic elements in the progress of these contextual analyses is the usage of man-made consciousness (simulated intelligence) and AI calculations. Businesses are able to process large amounts of data more effectively thanks to these technologies, which also allow them to accurately predict user preferences and patterns. The cooperative energy among innovation and personalization enables organizations to convey custom-made encounters at scale, driving consumer loyalty and devotion.

Past the purchaser confronting businesses, B2B organizations have likewise tackled the force of personalization. AI-driven personalization is used by Salesforce, a market leader in customer relationship management (CRM), to improve the user experience within its platform. By understanding client conduct, Salesforce tailors the point of interaction, proposes applicable elements, and furnishes bits of knowledge that line up with individual client jobs, at last expanding client reception and fulfillment.

Personalization has also changed the game when it comes to email marketing. For a situation study including clothing retailer ASOS, the execution of customized email crusades prompted a critical expansion in open rates and navigate rates. ASOS delivered targeted content that resonated with each customer segment by segmenting their audience based on preferences, purchase history, and browsing behavior. This improved engagement and conversion rates.

The outcome of these contextual analyses highlights the significance of a client driven approach in the period of computerized showcasing. Beyond simply addressing customers by their first name, personalization includes figuring out their inclinations, expecting their necessities, and conveying custom-made encounters across different touchpoints. As innovation keeps on advancing, organizations should adjust and use the capacities of artificial intelligence, AI, and information examination to remain ahead in the cutthroat scene.

Taking everything into account, the effect of fruitful contextual analyses on personalization advertising is significant and sweeping. Businesses in a variety of industries, including e-commerce giants like Amazon and Netflix and niche players like Stitch Fix, have reaped the benefits of providing personalized customer experiences. The consistent idea among these examples of overcoming adversity is the essential utilization of innovation, information examination, and a certified obligation to understanding and meeting individual client needs. Businesses that prioritize and invest in personalization will likely stand out in a crowded market as personalization continues to evolve, resulting in stronger connections with their target audience and long-term success.

Lessons Learned from Successful Implementations

Fruitful executions of personalization advertising have uncovered important illustrations that can direct organizations in upgrading client encounters and driving commitment. Personalization has turned into a foundation In present day promoting techniques, permitting brands to associate with their crowd on a more individualized level. Here are key illustrations gained from effective executions of personalization advertising:

Get to Know Your Target Market:
A thorough comprehension of your intended audience is the first step toward successful personalization. Dissect information to distinguish client

inclinations, ways of behaving, and socioeconomics. You can tailor marketing messages and experiences to meet the needs and interests of your audience by learning about them. When it feels relevant and in line with the individual's preferences, personalization is most effective.

Privacy and data quality are crucial:

While personalization depends vigorously on information, focusing on information quality and privacy is pivotal. Effective executions figure out the fragile harmony among personalization and regarding clients' security. Acquire express assent for information utilization, secure client data, and guarantee consistency with information assurance guidelines. Building entrust with clients is critical to supporting long haul customized connections.

Make use of AI and advanced analytics:

Effective personalization frequently influences progressed examination and man-made reasoning (computer based intelligence) calculations. Marketers can now deliver personalized content, recommendations, and offers thanks to these technologies, which make it possible to analyze huge datasets in real time. Carrying out man-made intelligence driven personalization improves versatility and accuracy, guaranteeing that proposals become more precise over the long haul as the framework gains from client corporations.

Division for Designated Personalization:

When personalization is done well, not all customers are treated the same.

Portion your crowd in light of different measures like socioeconomics, buying conduct, and inclinations. By making designated portions, you can fit personalization endeavors to explicit gatherings, expanding the importance of your showcasing messages and further developing general consumer loyalty.

Omnichannel Personalization:

Implementations that are successful acknowledge that customers interact with brands through multiple channels. Guarantee a consistent and predictable customized insight across different touchpoints, including sites, versatile applications, web-based entertainment, and email. Customers will always receive consistent and individualized messages through an omnichannel strategy, regardless of the platform they choose.

Adaptive Content Personalization:

Personalization goes past tending to clients by their most memorable name. Dynamic substance customization includes fitting the whole content of a message or website page in view of individual inclinations. Implementations that are successful make use of dynamic content to highlight deals, products, and recommendations that are tailored to each customer's specific interests, resulting in an experience that is more engaging and pertinent.

Beyond   transactions, personalization:

While personalization frequently begins with conditional corporations, effective executions broaden personalization past buy history. Comprehend and use information connected with client commitment, pursuing conduct, and social collaborations. By customizing the whole client venture, from attention to post-buy, brands can construct more grounded associations and encourage faithfulness.

Persistent Testing and Improvement:

Personalization is an iterative cycle. Personalization strategies are refined through continuous testing and optimization in successful implementations. A/B testing, multivariate testing, and examining client input assist with recognizing what turns out best for various fragments. By embracing a culture of trial and error, organizations can remain deft and adjust to developing client inclinations.

Offsetting Mechanization with Human Touch:

While robotization and simulated intelligence assume a critical part in personalization, effective executions comprehend the significance of keeping a human touch. Make progress toward a harmony between robotized personalization endeavors and human communication. Customized messages that pass on vagueness and compassion resound more with clients, adding to a positive brand discernment.

Estimating and Exhibiting return on initial capital investment:

Successful implementations regularly measure the return on investment (ROI) and establish key performance indicators (KPIs) to justify the investment in personalization. The results of personalized marketing efforts can be seen in metrics like higher customer lifetime value, increased conversion rates, and increased customer satisfaction.

All in all, fruitful executions of personalization showcasing highlight the significance of figuring out your crowd, focusing on information quality and security, utilizing trend setting innovations, and taking on a comprehensive, client driven approach. By embracing these examples, organizations can make customized encounters that drive commitment and steadfastness as well as add to long haul brand outcomes in an always developing computerized scene.

Chapter 7
Future Trends in Personalizatio n

Personalization is developing quickly, molding the manner in which people collaborate with items, administrations, and content. As innovation propels, future patterns in personalization are ready to rethink client encounters and change different ventures.

One key pattern is the ascent of hyper-personalization, where simulated intelligence calculations influence immense measures of information to make exceptionally customized encounters. This goes past essential segment data, integrating client conduct, inclinations, and even feelings. For example, online business stages might investigate past buys, perusing history, and virtual entertainment communications to prescribe items exceptionally fit to a singular's taste. This degree of personalization upgrades client commitment and fulfillment, encouraging long haul client connections.

Expanded reality (AR) and computer generated reality (VR) are likewise ready to assume a huge part in personalization. These advancements empower vivid, customized encounters, for example, virtual attempts for attire or customized virtual voyages through land properties. By mixing the computerized and actual universes, AR and VR improve personalization in manners beforehand, furnishing clients with a more intuitive and drawing in venture.

Voice and normal language handling (NLP) are vital parts of future personalization patterns. Voice-enacted gadgets and remote helpers are turning out to be progressively pervasive, permitting clients to connect with innovation through normal language. Systems are able to comprehend user intent, sentiment, and context as NLP capabilities advance, resulting in responses that are more precise and individualized. This pattern stretches out past brilliant speakers to applications in client care, content proposal, and even medical services interfaces.

Blockchain innovation is another component forming the fate of personalization. It tends to protection worries by permitting clients to have more noteworthy command over their information. With blockchain, people can concede particular admittance to their own data, guaranteeing that main significant gatherings can use it. This improves trust among clients and stages, encouraging a more straightforward and secure personalization environment.

Prescient investigation will keep on refining personalization techniques. AI algorithms can anticipate user needs and preferences and provide personalized recommendations in real time by analyzing historical data and user behavior patterns. This proactive methodology improves client fulfillment as well as adds to expanded transformation rates for organizations.

The Web of Things (IoT) is making a consistent trap of interconnected gadgets, further upgrading personalization prospects. Brilliant homes, wearable gadgets, and associated vehicles produce an abundance of information that can be utilized to make customized encounters. For instance, a shrewd home framework can gain proficiency with a singular's everyday daily practice and change lighting, temperature, and different inclinations in like manner.

Moral contemplations in personalization will turn out to be more unmistakable. As personalization innovations become more complex, issues connected with security, assent, and the capable utilization of information will come to the very front. Finding some kind of harmony between giving customized encounters and regarding client protection will be vital for organizations and innovation designers.

Personalization in training is an arising pattern that designers growth opportunities to individual understudies. Versatile learning stages use simulated intelligence to comprehend understudies' assets and shortcomings, changing coursework to oblige different learning styles. This approach guarantees that every understudy gets customized training, improving their learning process.

In the medical services area, personalization is changing patient consideration. Wearable gadgets and wellbeing applications gather constant information, permitting medical care suppliers to offer customized therapy plans and mediations. This pattern stretches out to genomics, where customized medication use a person's hereditary data to tailor clinical medicines for improved adequacy.

The joining of personalization in happy creation is developing, with simulated intelligence calculations helping with producing customized content in view of client inclinations. This incorporates customized news sources, music playlists, and even video suggestions. Content makers and stages are utilizing personalization to catch and hold client consideration in a profoundly serious computerized scene.

As personalization turns out to be more pervasive, the job of client assent and command over private information will be accentuated. Administrative systems will probably advance to guarantee that clients reserve the option to oversee and comprehend how their information is used for personalization purposes. Straightforwardness in information practices will be critical for keeping up with trust among clients and the stages they cooperate with.

All in all, the fate of personalization is dynamic and diverse, driven by headways in innovation and changing client assumptions. Hyper-personalization, vivid innovations, voice and NLP, blockchain, prescient investigation, IoT, moral contemplations, customized instruction, medical care change, and simulated intelligence driven content creation are adding to a scene where custom-made encounters are the standard. Finding some kind of harmony among personalization and security will be fundamental for guaranteeing the capable and economical advancement of customized advancements in the years to come.

Emerging Technologies Impacting Personalization

Arising innovations are essentially molding the scene of personalization across different ventures. Businesses are now able to tailor experiences on an unprecedented scale thanks to cutting-edge tools and advancements as we move through the digital age. From computerized reasoning (simulated intelligence) to expanded reality (AR), these innovations are reclassifying the manner in which we cooperate with items, administrations, and content.

One of the vital participants in personalization is computer based intelligence. AI calculations break down immense measures of information, empowering organizations to figure out client inclinations, ways of behaving, and designs. This profound comprehension considers profoundly designated proposals, whether it's recommending films on streaming stages or items on internet business sites. Artificial intelligence driven personalization improves client fulfillment as well as adds to expanded commitment and change rates.

In the domain of online business, remote helpers fueled by normal language handling (NLP) are turning out to be progressively refined. These AI-driven chatbots talk to users in real time, giving them personalized recommendations, responding to questions, and helping them make purchases. The capacity to comprehend and answer regular language causes these menial helpers to feel more human-like, making a more customized and connected shopping experience.

Expanded the truth is another innovation causing disturbances in personalization. In the retail area, AR permits clients to essentially take a stab at dress, extras, or even furniture prior to making a buy. By allowing customers to visualize products in their own environment, this immersive experience boosts personalization, significantly lowering the likelihood of returns and increasing customer satisfaction.

Emerging technologies are also transforming personalized health. Wearable gadgets furnished with sensors can gather constant information on a singular's wellbeing measurements, for example, pulse, rest designs, and active work. Computer based intelligence calculations break down this information to give customized wellbeing suggestions, from tweaked wellness schedules to updates for medicine. This degree of personalization further develops in general wellbeing results as well as enables people to play a more dynamic job in dealing with their prosperity.

The ascent of the Web of Things (IoT) is further adding to personalization across different spaces. Shrewd homes, for instance, influence IoT gadgets to learn client inclinations and mechanize errands, for example, changing lighting, temperature, and theater setups. This consistent coordination establishes a climate customized to the singular's propensities and inclinations, improving solace and proficiency.

In the field of advertising, customized content conveyance is arriving at new levels with the assistance of arising advancements. Man-made intelligence controlled content suggestion motors investigate client conduct and inclinations to present pertinent articles, recordings, or ads. This increments client commitment as well as upgrades promoting spend by focusing on people bound to be keen on unambiguous items or administrations.

Blockchain innovation is likewise assuming a part in personalization, especially in information security and protection. As clients become more mindful of the worth of their own information, blockchain offers a decentralized and secure method for overseeing and control admittance to this data. This expanded command over private information engages people to share just the data they are OK with, cultivating a feeling of confidence in web-based corporations.

Personalization is stretching out past the advanced domain with the approach of 3D printing. Customization of items, from customized cell phone cases to tailor made furnishings, is currently more available. This innovation permits buyers to be effectively associated with the plan cycle, bringing about extraordinary, exceptional things that resound with their own preferences and inclinations.

Be that as it may, with the horde advantages of arising advancements in personalization, moral contemplations and protection concerns come to the front. The assortment and use of immense measures of individual information bring up issues about assent, straightforwardness, and the potential for abuse. It is essential to strike a balance between personalization and protecting user privacy if these technologies are to be used responsibly and ethically.

Taking everything into account, the effect of arising advancements on personalization is significant and expansive. From artificial intelligence driven suggestions and increased reality in online business to customized wellbeing experiences from wearable gadgets, these advancements are reshaping the way that people communicate with the computerized and actual universes. To ensure a positive and responsible impact on individuals and society as a whole, it is essential to prioritize ethical considerations and strike a balance between personalization and privacy as we navigate this technologically advanced era.

Anticipated Changes in Consumer Expectations

Buyer assumptions are dynamic, continually developing because of innovative progressions, cultural moves, and market patterns. A number of anticipated shifts in consumer expectations are poised to reshape the landscape of businesses in a variety of industries going forward.

One critical shift rotates around the developing interest for consistent computerized encounters. With the multiplication of cell phones and fast web, purchasers anticipate that organizations should give frictionless internet based communications. To meet these expectations, businesses need to prioritize and invest in their digital presence, whether it's a user-friendly mobile app, a smooth e-commerce transaction, or effective customer service through digital channels.

Personalization is another key viewpoint that is progressively turning into a non-debatable assumption for buyers.

Propels in information examination and man-made consciousness engage organizations to figure out individual inclinations and ways of behaving. Customers expect individualized experiences as a result, including personalized product recommendations and marketing messages. Brands that can convey customized connections will probably acquire an upper hand in cultivating client dependability.

The idea of manageability is likewise acquiring unmistakable quality in customer assumptions. As ecological mindfulness develops, buyers are more aware of the effect their buying choices have in the world. They anticipate that organizations should take on eco-accommodating practices, lessen carbon impressions, and embrace reasonable obtaining and creation strategies. Organizations that incorporate supportability into their tasks are probably going to draw in naturally cognizant purchasers and upgrade their image notoriety.

Besides, the speed of conveyance has turned into a basic variable impacting shopper assumptions, especially in the online business area. Customers now expect expedited and dependable shipping services because of the proliferation of options for same-day and next-day delivery. These expectations will be met, and businesses that can provide quick and effective delivery methods may also gain a competitive advantage in the market.

Straightforwardness is arising as a foundation of customer trust, and assuming a considerably more huge part in the future is normal. Buyers need to know the starting points of items, comprehend the assembling processes, and be educated about the moral works regarding the organizations they support. Organizations that focus on straightforwardness in their activities and correspondence are probably going to construct more grounded associations with their client base.

The ascent of the membership economy is additionally forming shopper assumptions. Membership based models give comfort and a feeling of coherence for customers, who currently anticipate that organizations should offer membership choices for different items and administrations. This shift difficulties conventional plans of action, inciting organizations to investigate membership based contributions to line up with developing customer inclinations.

As innovation keeps on propelling, the reconciliation of increased reality (AR) and computer generated reality (VR) is expected to impact purchaser assumptions. The way consumers shop and experience products could be transformed by these immersive technologies. Organizations that embrace AR and VR to improve the web based shopping experience might acquire an upper hand by giving a really captivating and intuitive climate for purchasers.

The changing segment scene is likewise adding to shifts in purchaser assumptions. More youthful ages, like Twenty to thirty year olds and Age Z, focus on values like credibility, social obligation, and inclusivity. Organizations that adjust their informing and activities to these qualities are probably going to reverberate all the more unequivocally with these customer fragments.

Additionally, the post-pandemic era has accelerated the adoption of flexible and remote work arrangements, influencing customer expectations regarding accessibility and convenience. Items and administrations that take care of the necessities of people telecommuting or those with adaptable ways of life are supposed to be sought after.

All in all, expecting and adjusting to changes in buyer assumptions is pivotal for organizations to remain significant and serious. From advanced encounters to supportability, personalization, straightforwardness, and arising advances, organizations that proactively satisfy developing purchaser needs are ready to flourish in the unique commercial center representing things to come.

Chapter 8 Implementatio n Strategies

Personalization showcasing is a strong methodology that designers content and encounter to individual shoppers in view of their inclinations, ways of behaving, and socioeconomics. Effective execution requires an essential methodology that includes different components to make significant associations with clients. Here are key execution systems for successful personalization showcasing:

1. Information Assortment and Examination:

Begin by social event applicable client information, including socioeconomics, buy history, and online way of behaving.

Use progressed examination apparatuses to get noteworthy bits of knowledge from the gathered information.

Create targeted personalization strategies by gaining an understanding of the preferences, issues, and motivations of customers.

2. Segmentation:

Partition your crowd into portions in light of shared attributes or ways of behaving.

Tailor messages and contributions to each portion, guaranteeing that personalization is applicable to the particular necessities and interests of each gathering.

Consistently update and refine sections as client inclinations develop.

3. Conduct Following:

Execute apparatuses that track client conduct across different touchpoints.

Break down how clients interface with your site, messages, and different channels to expect their requirements.

Utilize constant conduct information to convey customized content at the right second in the client venture.

4. Content that Changes:

Make dynamic substance that adjusts to individual client qualities and conduct.

Utilize real-time data to tailor website content, emails, and product recommendations.

A/B test various varieties of customized content to improve commitment and transformation rates.

5. Customized Suggestions:

Influence AI calculations to create customized item or content suggestions.

Consider factors like past buys, perusing history, and inclinations to propose significant things.

Put in place recommendation engines that constantly learn from and adjust to the actions of customers.

6. Email Personalization:

Modify email crusades in light of individual inclinations and ways of behaving.

Utilize dynamic substance in messages to show customized item suggestions, elite offers, or significant substance.

Execute set off messages in view of explicit client activities or achievements.

7. Personalization on Mobile:

Streamline the portable involvement in customized content and offers.

Use area based focusing to convey pertinent messages in light of a client's geological area.

Maintain a consistent and individualized user experience by ensuring a seamless transition between various devices.

8. Personalized Websites:

Create landing pages that respond to user preferences in real time.

Tailor titles, pictures, and invitations to take action to line up with the guest's advantages and inclinations.

Lead A/B testing to refine and improve customized greeting page components.

9.   Virtual   Entertainment Personalization:

Personalize advertisements and content by utilizing social media data.

Make designated messages in light of client interests, commitment history, and segment data.

Execute social listening apparatuses to figure out client feelings and change personalization procedures as needs be.

10. Client Criticism and Overviews:

Assemble input to comprehend how clients see customized encounters.

Carry out studies to gather experiences on personalization viability and regions for development.

Follow up on input to refine and improve personalization techniques over the long haul.

11. Protection and Straightforwardness:

Focus on client security and guarantee consistency with information insurance guidelines.

Obviously convey to clients how their information will be utilized for personalization.

Make it possible for customers to choose how much personalization they receive by offering opt-in and opt-out options.

12. Ceaseless Improvement:

Carry out a nonstop improvement cycle, consistently surveying the presentation of personalization endeavors.

Test new personalization techniques and advancements to remain in front of developing client assumptions.

Stay adaptable and modify strategies in response to new trends and feedback from customers.

All in all, fruitful execution of personalization showcasing requires a comprehensive methodology that consolidates information driven experiences, dynamic substance creation, and a pledge to progressing improvement. Businesses can provide personalized experiences that foster stronger connections, increase customer loyalty, and drive business growth by comprehending customer behaviors, preferences, and expectations.

Steps to Implement Personalization in Marketing

Businesses that want to increase customer engagement and enhance the customer experience must incorporate personalization into their marketing strategies. Customized advertising permits organizations to tailor their messages, items, and administrations to individual inclinations, improving the probability of drawing in and holding clients. Here are key stages to execute personalization in your showcasing methodology really:

Get to Know Your Target Market:
Start by social affairs with extensive information on your interest group. Demographics, purchase history, browsing habits, and any other pertinent data should be examined. The basis for targeted marketing campaigns will be these data.

Put resources into Information Assortment and Examination Instruments:
Use progressed information assortment apparatuses and examination stages to assemble, process, and decipher client

data. These instruments can give significant experiences into client conduct, inclinations, and examples, empowering you to make more exact and successful customized crusades.

Characterize Client Fragments:

Divide your audience into distinct subsets based on shared traits, preferences, or behaviors. This division takes into consideration more designated and significant personalization. For instance, you could make sections for first-time purchasers, steadfast clients, or those inspired by unambiguous item classes.

Influence Client Relationship The board (CRM) Frameworks:

Executing a vigorous CRM framework can incorporate client information and work with a bound together perspective on every client's connections with your image. CRM frameworks empower customized correspondence by following client touchpoints and guaranteeing a consistent encounter across different channels.

Use Social Following:

Screen client conduct across computerized stages. Track site visits, email collaborations, and online entertainment commitment to acquire bits of knowledge into individual inclinations and propensities. This constant information takes into account dynamic and convenient personalization.

Make Customized Content:

Foster substance that resounds with every client section. Tailor messages, advancements, and item proposals in light of the particular interests and needs of each gathering. Your communication will be more likely to convert if it is relevant and engaging as a result of this.

Execute Dynamic Site Personalization:

Use innovation to customize the internet based insight for every guest. Carry out powerful happiness on your site that adjusts in light of the client's way of behaving, like appearance, customized item proposals, designated advancements, or applicable blog entries.

Email Personalization:

Addressing recipients by name and tailor content to their preferences are two ways to personalize email campaigns. Use robotization to send customized suggestions, selective offers, and pertinent updates in light of past collaborations.

Convey Customized Promotion Missions:

Influence the force of designated publicizing by making customized promotion crusades. Use client information to serve advertisements that line up with individual inclinations, improving the probability of snaps and transformations.

Execute Customized Suggestions:

Use recommendation engines to make content or product recommendations based on how each user behaves on your online platforms. Whether it's a "Suggested for You" segment on your site or customized playlists, these proposals improve the client experience.

Enhance Personalization on Mobile Devices:

Make sure your personalization efforts extend to mobile platforms in light of the growing use of mobile devices. Consider user behavior on mobile devices and smaller screen sizes when optimizing your mobile app and website for personalized experiences.

A/B Testing for Personalization Procedures:

Carry out A/B testing to survey the viability of various personalization methodologies. Explore different avenues regarding varieties in happiness, informing, and suggestions to recognize the most effective methodologies for every client section.

Protection and Security Contemplations:

Give data security and customer privacy top priority. Obviously convey how client information is utilized, acquire assent for personalization endeavors, and consent to pertinent information security guidelines to construct entrust with your crowd.

Continuous Improvement and Monitoring:

Personalization is a process that never ends. Routinely screen the presentation of your customized crusades, break down client input, and adjust your procedures in light of advancing inclinations and market patterns.

Businesses can develop a customized marketing strategy that boosts customer satisfaction, encourages brand loyalty, and drives long-term success by following these steps. Recollect that personalization is tied in with building significant associations with clients, and a first rate technique can separate your image in the present cutthroat commercial center.

Overcoming Common Implementation Challenges

For achieving desired outcomes, projects, strategies, or solutions must be effectively implemented. Notwithstanding, associations frequently experience different difficulties that can block the effective execution of plans. Perceiving and tending to these normal execution challenges is fundamental for guaranteeing smooth advancement and extreme achievement.

One of the essential obstacles in execution is deficient preparation. Plans that are too vague can cause problems like scope creep, delays, and confusion. To defeat this test, associations ought to concentrate on complete preparation, including characterizing clear goals, making sensible courses of events, and distinguishing possible dangers. A thoroughly examined plan fills in as a guide, directing the group through each period of execution and limiting vulnerabilities.

Another common obstacle that organizations frequently encounter during implementation is resistance to change. Individuals normally will generally oppose new cycles or advancements, dreading interruptions to their everyday practice. To beat opposition, powerful openness is absolutely vital. Pioneers ought to obviously explain the purposes for the change, underlining the advantages for both the association and people. Including key partners right off the bat simultaneously, tending to worries, and giving sufficient preparation can assist with cultivating an inspirational perspective toward change.

Lacking assets represent a huge impediment to effective execution. Whether it's spending plan requirements, a deficiency of talented faculty, or insufficient innovation, asset constraints can block progress. Before beginning implementation, organizations should conduct thorough resource assessments and allocate resources wisely. Focusing on undertakings, utilizing existing assets, and investigating coordinated effort open doors can assist with moderating asset limitations.

Ineffectively characterized jobs and obligations frequently lead to disarray and shortcomings during execution. For productive collaboration, it is essential to clearly define reporting structures, define each team member's responsibilities, and establish channels for communication. Standard registrations and updates guarantee everybody is in total agreement, encouraging a feeling of responsibility and cooperation.

Absence of partner commitment is a typical entanglement that can subvert execution endeavors. Partners, including representatives, clients, and accomplices, assume a crucial part in the outcome of any drive. Associations ought to effectively include partners from the arranging stage, looking for their feedback and tending to worries.

Consistent commitment all through the execution interaction helps fabricate a feeling of pride and guarantees that the arrangement addresses the issues of those it is planned to serve.

Unanticipated outside factors, like changes in guidelines or financial movements, can disturb execution plans. While it's difficult to anticipate each outside impact, associations can incorporate adaptability into their arrangements to adjust to unforeseen conditions. Consistently checking the outer climate and having emergency courses of action set up can assist associations with exploring unanticipated difficulties and change their execution techniques in a similar manner.

Insufficient correspondence is an unavoidable issue that can prompt false impressions and task disappointments. Powerful correspondence includes passing on data as well as guaranteeing that it is perceived. Using different correspondence channels, giving customary updates, and making an open criticism circle add to a straightforward and informed execution process. This incorporates resolving any arising issues immediately and changing the course depending on the situation.

Estimating and showing progress is significant for keeping up with energy and getting continuous help. Without clear measurements and detailing components, following the outcome of an execution effort can be challenging. Insights can be gained by establishing key performance indicators (KPIs) and regularly assessing progress in relation to these benchmarks. Straightforward announcing additionally helps in settling on informed choices, changing systems, and praising accomplishments, accordingly making everyone feel significantly better and responsibility.

Lastly, a feedback loop can prevent ongoing improvement. Associations ought to lay out components for gathering input from different partners all through the execution cycle. This information can distinguish regions for development, feature unanticipated difficulties, and proposition significant bits of knowledge for future activities. A culture of persistent improvement cultivates flexibility and versatility, situating the association for long haul achievement.

All in all, defeating normal execution challenges requires an all encompassing methodology that tends to arranging, correspondence, asset portion, partner commitment, flexibility, and nonstop improvement. By proactively distinguishing and moderating these difficulties, associations can improve the probability of effective execution and accomplish their ideal results.

Chapter 9 Measuring Personalizatio n Success

In the consistently developing scene of computerized encounters, personalization has arisen as a vital methodology for organizations looking to connect with and hold their crowd. Whether it's fitting site content, email missions, or item proposals, personalization expects to make a more individualized and significant experience for clients. However, robust success metrics must be established in order to guarantee the effectiveness of personalization efforts.

1. Client Commitment Measurements:
In the end, personalization is all about deeper user engagement. Measurements, for example, navigate rates, time spent nearby, and cooperation recurrence can give significant bits of knowledge into how well your customized content resounds with your crowd. Dissecting these measurements after some time permits organizations to check the effect of personalization endeavors on client commitment.

2. Transformation Rates:
The essential objective of personalization is frequently to drive

changes. Following change rates for customized encounters contrasted with nonexclusive ones can feature the viability of customized content in affecting client conduct. This can be used to achieve a variety of conversion objectives, including making a purchase, signing up for a newsletter, or completing a form.

3. Division Investigation:

Effective personalization depends on precise division of the crowd. Dissecting the exhibition of customized content across various sections gives bits of knowledge into which client bunches answer best to explicit personalization procedures. This data can help refine targeting and increase overall effectiveness by influencing future personalization decisions.

4. Personalization Effect on Income:

A basic measurement for organizations is the effect of personalization on income. This requires not only comprehending the long-term customer value but also tracking the direct revenue generated by personalized campaigns. By estimating the expansion in normal exchange worth and client lifetime esteem coming about because of personalization, organizations can survey the genuine monetary effect of their endeavors.

5. Consumer loyalty Overviews:

Direct criticism from clients is important. Carrying out consumer loyalty studies that explicitly address personalization encounters can give subjective bits of knowledge into client inclinations and discernments. Personalization strategies can be modified and enhanced by comprehending how audiences perceive personalized content.

6. Personalization Calculation Execution:

For stages using AI calculations for personalization, evaluating the presentation of these calculations is urgent. Measurements like exactness, accuracy, and review can assist with assessing how well the calculation predicts client inclinations. Constant observing and refinement of these calculations are fundamental for guaranteeing that customized proposals stay important and successful.

7. Cross-Channel Consistency:

In an omnichannel climate, personalization ought to offer a predictable encounter across different touchpoints. Measurements following the consistency of customized content and proposals across channels assist with guaranteeing a consistent and firm client venture. Errors in personalization methodologies between channels can prompt disarray and decrease the general effect.

8. A/B Testing:

A/B testing is a crucial technique for surveying the viability of personalization procedures. By contrasting the presentation of customized and non-customized varieties of content or missions, organizations can distinguish what reverberates best with their crowd. A/B testing gives an information driven way to deal with enhancing personalization endeavors in light of genuine client conduct.

9. Personalization Reaction Time:

The speed at which personalization is conveyed is urgent. A user's experience can be subpar as a result of slow response times. The efficiency of personalization as a whole is enhanced by monitoring the time it takes to display personalized content or generate recommendations. This ensures that users receive relevant information promptly.

10. Protection and Trust Measurements:

Personalization requires the collection and use of user data, so privacy and establishing trust with the audience must be taken into account. Personalization strategies' ethical implementation can be evaluated using metrics such as user opt-ins, comprehension of privacy policies, and trust indicators. Laying out and keeping up with trust is fundamental for long haul achievement.

All in all, estimating personalization achievement requires a complex methodology that envelops both quantitative and subjective measurements. By examining client commitment, change rates, division information, income influence, client criticism, calculation execution, cross-channel consistency, A/B testing results, reaction times, and security measurements, organizations can acquire an exhaustive comprehension of how well their personalization endeavors are resounding with their crowd. Constant observing and variation in light of these measurements are vital to remaining ahead in the unique scene of customized advanced encounters.

Key Performance Indicators (KPIs) for Personalization

Key Execution Markers (KPIs) are fundamental measurements used to evaluate the viability and outcome of different business techniques, and personalization is no special case. In the domain of personalization, where fitting encounters to individual inclinations is foremost, checking explicit KPIs becomes pivotal to guarantee that endeavors are lined up with goals and conveying unmistakable outcomes.

1. Transformation Rates:

Transformation rates are principal KPIs for personalization endeavors. They measure the level of guests who make an ideal move, like making a buy or pursuing a help. The impact on user engagement and satisfaction can be assessed by comparing conversion rates prior to and following the implementation of personalization.

2. Navigate Rates (CTR):

CTR is a crucial metric that evaluates the viability of customized content in catching clients' consideration. A higher CTR demonstrates that customized proposals or content reverberate well with the crowd, prompting expanded client communication.

3. Consumer loyalty (CSAT):

Personalization ought to upgrade the general client experience. Checking CSAT gives important experiences into how well personalization endeavors are meeting client assumptions. Customer satisfaction data can be gathered through surveys and feedback mechanisms, allowing for ongoing improvement.

4. Standards for dependability:

Personalization expects to assemble long haul associations with clients. The ability of personalization strategies to keep customers engaged over time can be evaluated by monitoring retention rates. Customer loyalty is influenced by personalized experiences, as evidenced by a higher retention rate.

5. Normal Request Worth (AOV):

AOV estimates the typical sum spent by clients during an exchange. Personalization shouldn't just drive commitment yet additionally empower higher spending. Breaking down AOV when personalization executions assess the effect on income.

6. Personalization Viability Score:

Create a personalized effectiveness score that provides an overall evaluation of personalization efforts by combining various metrics. This score might incorporate variables like change rates, CTR, and consumer loyalty, giving an extensive perspective on the outcome of personalization techniques.

7. Division Exactness:

Compelling personalization depends on the exact division of the interest group. Personalized content is relevant and resonates with specific user groups if the accuracy of segmenting users based on their preferences and behavior is monitored.

8. Time on the Job:

Customized encounters ought to catch clients' consideration and support delayed communication. After personalization is implemented, it is helpful to assess the level of engagement as well as the impact on the user experience to monitor the average amount of time users spend on the website.

9. Rate of Bounce:

A high skip rate shows that guests are leaving the site rapidly without drawing in with the substance. Checking bob rates post-personalization can uncover whether the customized encounters are actually diminishing skip rates and empowering clients to investigate further.

10. Profit from Speculation (return on initial capital investment):

Evaluate the monetary effect of personalization endeavors by ascertaining the profit from the venture. This includes looking at the expenses of carrying out personalization procedures with the subsequent expansion in income or other characterized goals.

11. Strategically pitching and Up-Selling Measurements:

Personalization frequently includes suggesting extra items or administrations in light of client conduct. Observing the outcome of strategically pitching and up-selling endeavors gives experiences into the viability of customized ideas in driving extra buys.

12. Engagement of Users Through Personalization Features:

On the off chance that personalization highlights are coordinated into the UI, following client commitment with these elements is essential. This includes interactions with saved preferences, personalized recommendations, and any other features made to improve the user experience.

13. Content Viability:
Assess the exhibition of customized content by breaking down measurements intended for each sort of satisfaction. Metrics like open rates and click-through rates, for instance, offer insight into the efficiency of personalized emails that are a part of the strategy.

14. Portable Responsiveness:
With the rising utilization of cell phones, guaranteeing that personalization endeavors stretch out consistently to portable stages is fundamental. Checking versatile explicit KPIs, for example, portable change rates and portable commitment, improves the client experience across gadgets.

Ultimately, effective personalization extends beyond customization; it includes ceaselessly estimating and refining techniques to line up with client inclinations and business goals. By routinely observing these key execution pointers, organizations can acquire significant bits of knowledge into the effect of personalization endeavors and settle on information driven choices to improve the general client experience and drive manageable development.

Tools and Metrics for Evaluation

Devices and measurements assume an urgent part in the assessment cycle across different spaces, giving experiences into execution, proficiency, and generally speaking viability. The selection of appropriate tools and metrics is essential for making informed decisions and continuous improvement, regardless of whether they are implemented in technology, education, or business.

In the domain of business, execution assessment apparatuses are instrumental in evaluating the progress of key drives and functional proficiency. Key Execution Markers (KPIs) act as fundamental measurements, offering a quantifiable proportion of hierarchical execution. Measurements like income development, consumer loyalty, and worker efficiency empower organizations to keep tabs on their development and recognize regions for upgrade.

Monetary measurements, remembering Return for Speculation (return for capital invested) and overall revenues, are essential instruments for assessing the monetary soundness of a business. A comprehensive view of the efficiency with which resources are utilized and the venture's overall profitability is provided by these metrics. Furthermore, devices like adjusted scorecards coordinate different execution markers, offering a comprehensive viewpoint on hierarchical achievement.

For evaluating student learning outcomes and institutional effectiveness, evaluation tools and metrics are essential in the educational landscape. Government sanctioned tests and evaluations give quantifiable information on understudy execution, empowering instructors to fit helping strategies and educational plans to address explicit necessities.

Institutional metrics like graduation rates, retention rates, and alumni success are essential for assessing educational institutions' overall effectiveness. These metrics go beyond individual student assessment. These measurements assist partners with recognizing regions for development and check the foundation's effect on understudies' drawn out progress.

Software development is a field in which a variety of tools and metrics are used to guarantee the quality and effectiveness of the development process. Code audit instruments, for instance, empower designers to evaluate the nature of code, distinguish messes with, and guarantee adherence to coding principles. Persistent Reconciliation (CI) and Ceaseless Conveyance (Compact disc) instruments mechanize the testing and organization processes, smoothing out improvement work processes.

Measurements like code inclusion, bug thickness, and reaction time offer bits of knowledge into the exhibition and unwavering quality of programming applications. These metrics help development teams make decisions based on data to improve their products' overall quality. Client experience measurements, for example, bob rates and transformation rates, further add to the assessment interaction by surveying the viability and ease of use of programming connection points.

In medical services, apparatuses and measurements are fundamental for assessing the nature of patient consideration, functional proficiency, and by and large execution of medical care associations. Patient fulfillment studies give important input on the nature of care and patient encounters. Medical services suppliers additionally depend on clinical result measurements, for example, death rates and confusion rates, to evaluate the adequacy of clinical therapies and intercessions.

Proficiency measurements, for example, patient stand by times and asset usage, assist medical services associations with advancing their tasks and improve the general patient experience. Electronic Wellbeing Record (EHR) frameworks act as instruments that work with information assortment and investigation, permitting medical services experts to settle on informed choices and work on understanding results.

No matter what the business, the determination of fitting assessment apparatuses and measurements is critical for significant appraisals. To make sure that the tools chosen are in line with the desired outcomes, it is essential to consider the specific goals and objectives of the evaluation process. In addition, the persistent advancement of innovation presents new devices and measurements, expecting associations to remain versatile and embrace developments that upgrade their assessment abilities.

All in all, apparatuses and measurements are basic parts of the assessment cycle across different fields. Whether utilized in business, schooling, innovation, or medical services, these apparatuses give significant bits of knowledge into execution, productivity, and by and large adequacy. The cautious determination of fitting apparatuses and measurements empowers associations to settle on informed choices, drive persistent improvement, and accomplish their essential goals.

CONCLUSION

Key Points and Future Landscape of Personalization in Marketing

Personalization in showcasing is a dynamic and extraordinary power that has developed fundamentally throughout the long term. As we dig into the central issues and future scene of personalization in showcasing, it's fundamental to perceive its effect on buyer commitment, brand faithfulness, and in general business achievement.

One of the central parts of personalization is the capacity to tailor content and encounters in light of individual inclinations and ways of behaving. This designated approach upgrades consumer loyalty as well as encourages a more profound association between the brand and the buyer. The period of conventional mass showcasing is steadily disappearing, accounting for procedures that reverberate with the novel requirements and interests of every client.

The significance of data in personalization is a crucial point. With the approach of cutting edge investigation and AI, advertisers can use huge measures of information to acquire bits of knowledge into client conduct. From site communications to buy history, each touchpoint adds to a complete comprehension of the shopper. Nevertheless, it is essential to strike a balance between personalization and privacy while preserving individual preferences and boundaries.

Also, personalization stretches out past item proposals. Brands are currently zeroing in on fitting the whole client venture, from the underlying cooperation to post-buy commitment. This all encompassing methodology guarantees a consistent and customized insight at each stage, building up brand dependability and driving recurrent business.

One more key angle is the reconciliation of computerized reasoning (man-made intelligence) in personalization techniques. Man-made intelligence controlled calculations can break down information at scale, recognizing designs and anticipating future ways of behaving. This empowers constant personalization as well as works with expectant customization, where brands can proactively address client issues before they even express them. The constant progressions in simulated intelligence innovation guarantee a much more refined and nuanced level of personalization later on.

The ascent of omnichannel showcasing is additionally reshaping the scene of personalization. Customers today draw in with brands across different stages, including sites, web-based entertainment, portable applications, and coming up. Personalization endeavors should be flawlessly incorporated across these channels to give a steady and firm insight. The difficulty lies in ensuring that personalized interactions are synchronized across all touchpoints by developing a single view of the customer.

Moreover, personalization isn't restricted to B2C advertising; it is similarly essential in B2B conditions. Organizations are progressively perceiving the worth of customized correspondence and custom-made answers for their clients. The future scene of B2B personalization includes utilizing information driven experiences to grasp the exceptional difficulties and objectives of every business, consequently fortifying associations and driving shared accomplishment.

As we look into the fate of personalization in showcasing, a few patterns arise that will shape the scene before very long. Hyper-personalization is one such pattern, where brands go past essential division and designer encounters at a singular level. This includes utilizing constant information, simulated intelligence, and AI to convey profoundly customized content, suggestions, and advancements, making a balanced association with every client.

Voice and visual search are also expected to have a significant impact on personalization in the future. As additional customers embrace voice-enacted gadgets and visual hunt innovation, advertisers have the amazing chance to customize content in light of these corporations. Delivering individualized experiences through these emerging channels will require a thorough understanding of the nuances of voice commands and visual preferences.

The moral component of personalization can't be neglected later on. As personalization turns out to be more refined, worries about information security and assent will heighten. Brands that focus on straightforwardness and give shoppers command over their information will acquire trust and hang out in a climate where information assurance is fundamental.

All in all, the central issues of personalization in advertising revolve around information driven bits of knowledge, simulated intelligence coordination, omnichannel methodologies, and the development towards hyper-personalization. The future scene holds energizing possibilities, with headways in innovation empowering significantly more nuanced and individualized approaches. Brands that effectively explore the harmony among personalization and protection, embrace arising patterns, and focus on moral contemplations will be strategically set up to flourish in the always developing scene of customized showcasing.

DEAR READER

Your thoughts matter to us! If the book brought a smile or moment of respite, please Consider Sharing your experience through a review.

Your feedback is invaluable in making our book even more enjoyable to following.We hope this message finds you well and enjoy your literary adventures! We value the opinions of our readers, and we would love to hear your thoughts on **[PERSONALIZATION IN MARKETING]**.

Thank you for being a part of our literary journey, and we look forward to reading your review!

WARM REGARDS